The Pie Eating Man's Guide to a Healthy Mind

A book for everyday people like me

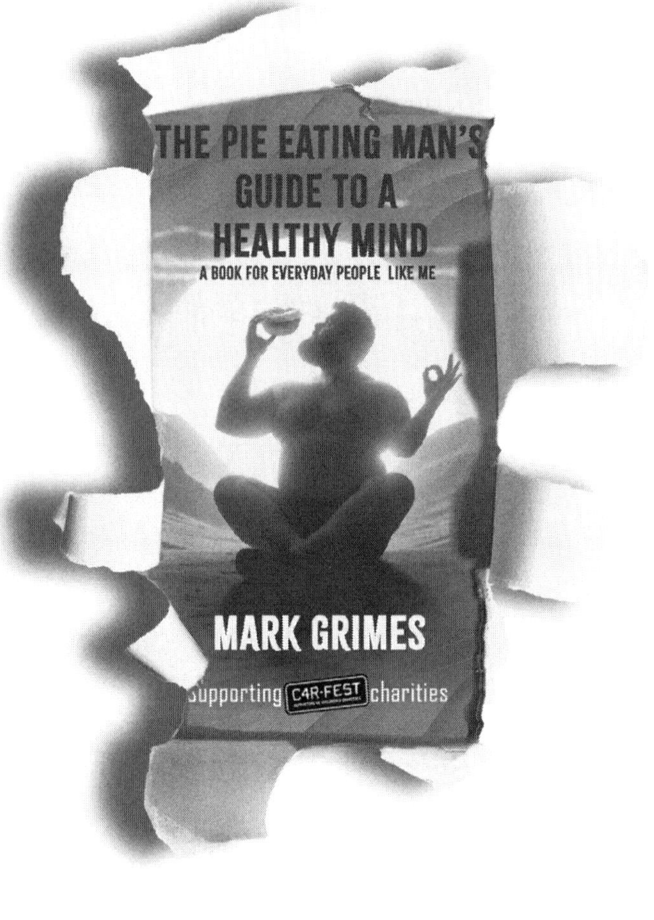

Supporting  charities

At least 10% of profits raised through the sale of this book, will be donated to the Charities chosen by CarFest.

Copyright © 2025 Mark Grimes.

All rights reserved.

Cover design by Mark Grimes

Book Cover design by Mark Grimes

Artwork in this book was created using Adobe Firefly or Bing AI image creator and edited or adapted by Mark Grimes.

No part of this book can be reproduced in any form or by written, electronic or mechanical, including photocopying, recording, or by any information retrieval system without written permission in writing by the author.

Edited by Corner House Words

www.cornerhousewords.co.uk

Although every precaution has been taken in the preparation of this book, the publisher and author assume no responsibility for errors or omissions. Neither is any liability assumed for damages resulting from the use of information contained herein.

Dedication

This book is dedicated to my wife Esther and my two boys Jordan and Max. My mum, all of my wonderful 'framily', Peps, O, Bobby, Nick W, Nick G, Jez the angry beaver, Betty P, Cpt. Mark, Silent Bob, Dave H, Auntie Gill, Uncle Geoff, Grandma and Grandad North and Grandma Grimes for seeing me through the dark times.

It is also dedicated to everyone who has offered supportive and encouraging words to me as I have been writing and banging on about this book over the past year, your kindness really has made a difference.

Foreword

I am a twenty stone; six-foot tall bloke (OK, I'm five foot eleven) who can look quite intimidating in a dark alley.

In the past, I have been the type of person who thought yoga is for middle-class folk who have endless time on their hands and that mindfulness and meditation are just for hippies. Not for people like me. I thought mental ill health was a weakness, something not to be shared with other people. But pushing myself out of my comfort zone and coming at things with an open mind has changed my point of view. After listening to people who I know have my best interests at heart, I have tried new ways of thinking and it has been incredibly good for me.

As a result, I have made wonderful new friends; I have improved my life and the lives of people around me. I WAS WRONG! So maybe you are too.

You don't have to have mental health problems to benefit from reading this book. There is something here for everyone if we open our minds to new approaches and ways of accepting who we are. I will share with you my experiences of depression, stress, anxiety, ADHD and grief, so that we can both become better informed on these subjects.

It is a collection of bits and bobs designed to get you thinking about how you can improve your life and the lives of those around you. Everyone has a comfort zone and I would love this book to support you in redefining yours and helping you to feel better.

Throughout the book, there are activities, practices and pieces of guidance to provide you with a toolkit, helping you to try new ways of thinking and manage your life in a less burdensome way.

I would love to think that the knowledge and experiences I have had could help others who are a bit like me. Maybe it could help them to lead a happier, more meaningful and mindful life.

Contents

Chapter	Chapter Title	Page
-	**Dedication**	-
-	**Foreword**	-
-	**Introducing the Pie Eating Man**	i
1	**The origins of this book**	1
	- My Black Dog - The man - Our brains belong to Neanderthals - The power of one	
2	**"Mental health is for flaky people, isn't it?"**	7
	- My mate Bob - Toxic masculinity - Does toxic masculinity breed more toxic masculinity? - Don't just stand there - How can we help people? - If nothing changes, it will remain the same - So what can we do about it?	
3	**My childhood**	17
	- Growing up a bit broken - The legacy of being a little s**t! - Boredom is underrated - Senior school	
4	**The 'B' word**	23

Chapter	Chapter Title	Page
	- Jesus sandals - What is bullying? - The definition of bullying - Protected characteristics - Am I a bully? - How can bullying impact on individuals - Dealing with bullies - Guidance for people being bullied in the workplace - Feeling bullied or harassed? What should you do? - Be the difference	
5	**My mental health**	35
	- Breakdowns and change - Fixed and Fluid self - Fixed self - Fluid self - The value of other people's views on you - A change is as good as a rest -Life pivots - My first trip abroad - Going to Uni - Breakdown #1	
6	**A new start**	47
	- The beginning of my new beginning - The Ramshill - Red Work - Breakdown #2	
7	**Let's get down to the nitty gritty!**	55
	- What is mental health? - What is mental 'ill' health? - What is mental 'wellbeing'? - How can mental ill health	

Chapter	Chapter Title	Page
	affect our day-to-day lives? - Mental health is like a housing estate - Common misconceptions associated with mental health issues - A whistlestop guide to mental health basics - Working to change mental health stereotypes - Communication is everything	
8	**Depression** - What is depression? - How depression affects me - Untangling the ball of string - Symptoms of depression - How does this differ from feeling down? - Some causes of depression - Other symptoms of depression - How our depression can affect those we care about most - Depression and the demands of daily life - Suicidal thoughts - The Pie Eating Man's approach to depression - Just take the "effing" tablets man!	65
9	**Stress** - What is stress? - Emotional hijack by our own brain!! - What causes stress? - Harmful effects of stress	79

Chapter	Chapter Title	Page
	- Positive effects of stress - Symptoms of stress - How does stress affect us? - Second hand stress	
10	**Anxiety**	87
	- What is anxiety? - What is a panic attack? - What causes anxiety? - Worry - Using anxiety to do good? - Manifestation - Be careful when using social media - Ways to manage anxiety - Give yourself space - How finding positives can help to reduce anxiety - Anxiety management activities - Time out - Talking therapy	
11	**Negativity**	97
	- Life is tough - Negative thoughts - What is negative bias? - Managing negative bias - Our inner voice is a $h17h34d! - Managing the $h17h34d - Imposter syndrome - Vortex of negative thinking - The curse of negativity - Remaining positive	
12	**Trauma and triggers**	105
	- Trauma before triggers - Trauma	

Chapter	Chapter Title	Page
	- Triggers	
13	**Attention Deficit Hyperactivity Disorder (ADHD)**	111
	- What is ADHD? - Who is likely to be diagnosed with ADHD? - What are the causes of ADHD? - How does ADHD affect us as Individuals? - How can ADHD affect those around us? - What are the symptoms associated with ADHD? - Complete the tasks you start - ADHS not ADHD – it's a superpower not a disorder - How can you help someone to manage their ADHD? - What help is out there? - Cognitive Behavioural Therapy (CBT) - ADHD and crappy food	
14	**Grief**	125
	- What is grief? - There is no right or wrong way to grieve - Poems, humour and my grandparent(s) - Grief management	
15	**The menopause**	135
	- Why is there a chapter on menopause in this book? - What is the menopause? - What is meant by the perimenopause?	

Chapter	Chapter Title	Page
	- What are the most common symptoms associated with perimenopause and menopause? - Why should we <u>ALL</u> be talking about it? - Everyone is affected, so everyone should help	
16	**Maintaining good mental health**	143
	- My mental health is my problem - Managing mental health is a journey not an action - Don't make money your priority - Honesty - Asking for help - There's no such thing as a bad idea - Seeking support from a counsellor or a talking therapist - The importance of happiness - Working from home - Take regular breaks from your desk - Keeping a stress journal - Be kind to yourself – learn to say no - Golden rule – never compare yourself to others - You are awesome! - Big G's Campaign for Positivity on Facebook - Who can you talk to? - Mental health can fluctuate	

Chapter	Chapter Title	Page
17	**The value of healthy routines in recovery** - Routine is key - Get up earlier - Get up early and go somewhere exciting - Make your bed - Wash up or empty the dishwasher - Make your own lunch - Try something new - Eat socially - Being 'present' or 'in the moment' while eating - Listen to music - Move your fruit bowl - My sock drawer - Keep your feet warm and dry - The value of routine in recovery - Maintain a healthy sleep routine - The pitfalls of the wrong routine	161
18	**Kindness, gratitude & forgiveness** - Humankind not Human-unkind - Kindness - The three states of gratitude and forgiveness - The three states of gratitude - The three states of forgiveness - Sorry is a much bigger word than you might expect - Sorry means nothing without change	173

Chapter	Chapter Title	Page
	- Talk to someone and make them smile - Emotional intelligence - Gratitude - Giving gratitude to those who deserve it - Do good things for others - Be kind to others - Give thanks for what you have - Look after those who look after you – don't be a Clasper	
19	**Meditation, mindfulness & remembering to breathe** - What is meditation? - The formal approach on how to meditate - Using meditation to train my ADHD - The Pie Eating Man's approach to meditation - What is visualisation meditation? - Mindfulness - Mindful breathing and breathwork - Scuba diving – breathing like your life depends on it - Breathwork - Nature has all you need, just open your senses - Other therapeutic activities - Relaxation - Yoga - Massage	189

Chapter	Chapter Title	Page
20	**Goals, bucket lists & plans** - Make plans long and short term - Write a bucket list or five - Short term achievable in a year - Life-time bucket list - Remembering bucket list items you have achieved - Revisiting the list - Local attraction bucket list - General rules for all five bucket lists - Have things in your diary to look forward to - Enjoy the build up	203
21	**Toolkit for a healthy mind** - My strengths and weaknesses - What makes you tick? What motivates you? - What makes you happy? - What made you tick as a kid? - Mental health and medication - Don't self-medicate with drugs and/or alcohol	211
22	**Getting to know You and helping yourself** - You owe it to yourself - Loyalty web - Faith and spiritualism - Change is our responsibility - My hobbies - You really do have time! - You just need to allocate it - Helping out and volunteering	217

Chapter	Chapter Title	Page
	- My theory on a sixth sense	
23	**How can I help someone else?**	229
	- Are you really ready? - How to help and what signs to look for - Useful tips to keep in mind - The Black Dog by Matthew Johnstone	
24	**NEWS Bulletins**	235
	- NEWS Bulletin #1 - NEWS Bulletin #2 - NEWS Bulletin #3 - NEWS Bulletin #4 - NEWS Bulletin #5 - NEWS Bulletin #6 - NEWS Bulletin #7 - NEWS Bulletin #8 - NEWS Bulletin #9 - NEWS Bulletin #10 - NEWS Bulletin #11 - NEWS Bulletin #12 - NEWS Bulletin #13 - NEWS Bulletin #14 - NEWS Bulletin #15 - NEWS Bulletin #16 - NEWS Bulletin #17 - NEWS Bulletin #18 - NEWS Bulletin #19	
25	**Your worksheets**	247
	- Your life pivots - Depression diary - Stress & triggers diary - List of change indicators (blank) - List of change indicators	

Chapter	Chapter Title	Page
	- Three things I'm grateful for today - Life time bucket list - Bucket list items achieved - Bucket list items to revisit - My joy and worry lists - My pros and cons	
26	I did a thing!!!	259
27	The photos	263
28	Helpful resources	271
-	Glossary of "woo woo" words and terms used in this book	279
-	The encore	289
-	About the author	291

Introducing The Pie Eating Man

I am active but overweight; have a mortgage and a hardworking credit card just like anyone else. I work full time and do not do enough exercise. My wife and I do our own decorating and we would like more holidays. I enjoy watching footy, but I am terrible at playing it.

A bit of a nerd, I play board games with my friends every week; we call this 'Nerd Club'; I like Star Wars and Lord of the Rings and all that jazz And I'm daft.

What I'm trying to say is that I'm a normal person; not a 'hippie', nor am I so wealthy that I don't have to worry about stuff. I like a beer and I eat pies. I don't think I'm any more important than the next person and I am very grateful for everything I have, especially my wonderful wife and two boys.

Maybe the only difference between you and me is that having suffered with depression from an early age, I have thought about it A LOT. I have also seen flashes of it in other people and recognise that by using the 'Power of One' (see chapter 1) and sharing my experiences with you, I might help you help yourself and others too.

I don't know how to write a book!

I am sitting in a camping chair in front of the stage area of CarFest 2022. I'm watching Ocean Colour Scene in a light drizzle, eating room temperature Red Leicester cheese and drinking a cup of shandy that I prepared in a lemonade bottle this morning (Ocean Colour Scene are rocking it by the way).

This afternoon I spoke with Suzy Izzard (better known as Eddie) and Chris Evans. I asked them how someone like me could write a book about the journey of discovery that I have embarked on, without a lot of technical knowledge on the subject and without ever having written more than a Christmas list. (See Photo 1 in the photos section)

Suzy told me that if I wanted to write a book, the only way to do it is to get on and write it. No matter what the subject, I needed to get out my laptop, or phone or notepad and just do it.

So here I am, just doing it. I am surrounded by good people, enjoying the music and the camaraderie offered by this excellent festival and it is inspiring me.

As I sit here, I am very aware that most books are written by writers and I am not one, or at least I wasn't until I started writing this. I am a decent communicator with a half decent grasp of English and able to write a decent letter, so what have I got to lose by giving it a go? I expect when/if I get to the end of the journey of writing this book, I may be able to answer that question.

A year later, I met Suzy again. I asked if she remembered me and my question from the year before, she said that she did and asked how it was going. Giving her an awkward glance, I confessed:

"I have only written a few hundred words" I said, explaining I had decided I needed to do further training on the subject and had undertaken some mental health courses and had been studying wellbeing.

Suzy is a highly intelligent person; she is very kind but doesn't suffer fools gladly. She is like a wise teacher or village elder. She gave me a sidewards glance and raised her eyebrow and said, "That's just prevarication, if you don't sit down and actually write the book, you can come up with as many excuses as you like, but you will not have a book to show for it." Suzy hit the nail on the head and this was the kick up the arse that I needed. (See Photo 3 in the photos section)

I still don't really know how to write a book though and I don't know how I can be sure if the book I write will be any good.

There's only one way to find out, I suppose...

How to read (this book)

I wanted to write the book in a way that you, the reader, can pick it up and put it down, flick through it and read short sections, not always in order, so that you can take snippets from it as and when it suits you. You don't have to put two hours aside to read it. Although you can if you feel so inclined!

I have ADHD, so I have a short attention span; I like to read in the manner that people speak, so I have tried to write this book in that way. A few years ago, while on holiday in Egypt, I read Shaun Ryder's autobiography "Twisting my melon". My wife, Esther, bought me the book for my birthday. Not only was it an excellent and honest account of his life, but it was written in this way and I couldn't put it down. I hope this works for you too or I might be done for.

The content of the book is structured to take you on a journey and I will share with you my experiences of my own mental health difficulties. We will look at some of the more common mental health factors and the disruption that can be caused to so many lives.

I will share some methods you can use to manage these issues and some solutions which should help you to lead a happier and more comfortable life alongside mental health.

The stories and examples that I have provided in relation to my life are not there because I believe I am interesting or important. In fact, quite the opposite. I'm no more interesting than the next person. I just hope my story shows how anybody can find themselves in a mess through no fault of their own. It doesn't always happen overnight because of one single event (although this is, of course, possible). It is normally a series of events and missed opportunities, which you might avoid with better awareness and increased understanding.

You could refer to this book as a 'bog book,' and I don't think that requires an explanation! It should be within easy reach, so you can grab it whenever needed. Just leave it some place where it will not be defiled and made unhygienic by a non-calibrated shot at the pan.

Just pick it up and read any section you fancy; there is useful advice and information available in every section of the book.

You will find that the same management method can be used to help with more than one mental health condition.

Try to remember this as you are going through the book. You may feel that although you primarily struggle with anxiety, a method used to help with stress is also useful to you. You may also find that when reading about different mental health conditions, you recognise symptoms associated with those too. Many of these conditions do overlap with one another.

This is your book, here's how to use it

Right then, now that you know how to read this book, here's how to use and abuse it.

You'll notice that at the end of each chapter, there's a blank page. That's not an error. It's not because I misjudged the printing layout or forgot to add something. It's there on purpose.

Why? Because this book isn't just for reading, it's for doing. You're encouraged (with absolutely no pressure) to scribble your thoughts, reactions, ideas or mini-rants on those blank pages. Make a plan, have a moan, write something beautiful, or just doodle something daft while the kettle's boiling. Whatever works for you.

Throughout the book, I've also included sample worksheets filled in with my own thoughts and feelings. These are here to show you how I've used the tools and exercises myself, warts and all. You might relate to some bits, or you might think I'm totally off my trolley. Either way, they're meant to help spark your own thinking.

When you reach Chapter 25, you'll find blank versions of each of those worksheets. They're yours. Tear them out, copy them, write all over them, fold them into paper aeroplanes if it helps — they're there to be used. Think of them as your own personal toolkit, ready for whenever you need it.

This is your book. Use it your way. Doodle in it. Spatter it with tea. Fill it with your real thoughts, because no one else has to read it unless you want them to.

The only rule? If it helps you feel a bit better, a bit stronger, or a bit more understood, you're using it exactly right.

WARNING!
Woo-woo alert!

Woo-woo; a phrase often used to describe things which may appear to be spiritual, or 'hippie' in their origins.

If you already have a negative or judgemental idea of mental health, wellness and mindfulness, there are phrases used in this book which have the potential to put you off.

Please, try to keep an open mind regarding this. After all, this forms the backbone of the book. Try not to judge too quickly as I promise the book is not judging you.

I may also use some unfamiliar woo-woo or mental health related words and phrases. To address this, I have included a glossary of some of those towards the end of the book, so you don't have to look like a plum and ask someone else what they mean.

Chapter 1
The origins of this book

My Black Dog

You may recognise this term associated with mental health. It was the term Winston Churchill used to describe his low moods and what we believe was depression. It is also the name of a mental health charity that I have been volunteering for over the past four years.

I first heard about the charity on the Chris Evans Breakfast Show on Virgin Radio. The patron of the charity, Eddy Temple Morris ran an auction with Chris's help. There were many cool items available, which focussed on rock and roll memorabilia and they raised thousands of pounds for the charity.

They described My black dog as a community focussed platform which offered a peer-to-peer chat-based system for people who were struggling with their mental health. All their volunteers had a history of mental health problems and they offered advice and a friendly ear to anyone who wanted to use their online chat system.

I wasn't in a financial position to bid for any of the items in the auction. However, I had some knowledge of mental health and have had my own issues. So, I contacted them and I have been volunteering for them ever since. Helping people you will never meet anonymously, when they are struggling with their mental health is an extremely rewarding experience and I am incredibly grateful for being given the opportunity by the charity.

You can find out more about them here on their website: www.MyBlackDog.co

The man

I first saw a need for this book back in 2022, while attending CarFest, a family friendly festival setup by radio personality Chris Evans, where I was volunteering on the My Black Dog stand.

A gentleman who had been listening to me talking about my mental health history came over to me and quietly asked if he could speak with me away from the stand. He was in his sixties, a down-to-earth bloke, a manual worker for the whole of his life who had recently retired. He was at the festival with his mates, to look at the amazing cars on show.

"How do I know if I am suffering with depression?" he asked.

This single question was so special. This man trusted me, a stranger, with the weight of such a serious matter and I knew it was my responsibility to share as much of the truth in relation to the subject as possible. In the end, we spoke for almost an hour about some indicators and symptoms related to depression and changes that it can cause in our lives. He told me he was happily married and loved his wife; he had good friends and was financially secure, but he explained that nobody in his life talked about these things. Up till now, he had not really considered it, but he thought he might have depression.

At the end of our conversation, he told me our chat had

brought him great comfort and relief. He identified with many of things we had discussed and was extremely grateful to have spoken about his situation. We ended our chat with a big hug. It was the kind of hug you have with a good mate and then he went off to find his friends.

I did not know his name and although I saw him again over the weekend to say 'Hi'; I have never seen him since.

Our interaction was so inspiring. He felt comfortable enough to speak up; we had time to talk in an environment he was comfortable with and I could share information with him which, hopefully, helped him to go away and seek some support that could improve his life.

This was the moment I began wondering how I could help other people like that chap. People who may be unhappy and may not realise that this is the case. They are not looking for support, so they may never find it.

I realised how important it is for us to be aware of ourselves and the things that affect us every day. I also realised that I have a responsibility to share my experience with as many people as I can, because I want to help them too.

Facing up to this stuff is one of the most difficult steps in this process; life does not come with a manual and even if it did, there would have to be a different one for every one of us. We are all unique and the issues that one person has absolutely no concerns about might be something that eats away at you every hour of every day.

Our brains belong to Neanderthals

Writing this book is important to me because I want to help people. Even more, I want to help people like me, to help themselves. For tens of thousands of years, we humans lived a simple life managing our food resources, worshiping our gods, trying our best to stay warm and dry and protecting our families and friends from sabre-toothed tigers or at the very least, really grumpy badgers. Over the past five hundred years, that lifestyle has changed beyond all recognition; modern life has managed our primal roles and responsibilities to a level that they are no longer there, particularly in the western world.

The world we live in is still tough, but the need to solve problems, to be physical, to find food and to worship has changed. Our entire lives are now much more convenient; however, it has happened so quickly that our brains and our bodies have not been able to adjust. They don't receive the inputs and stimuli they need or expect to function healthily or as they have evolved to.

There is no shame associated with understanding when we are struggling with our mental health and there should be no shame in seeking support with it. Unfortunately, society has created a narrative which suggests otherwise.

When I talk to people and they say they are ashamed or embarrassed about discussing their situation, I offer this example:

Let's imagine that you injured yourself playing sports when you were younger. The injury caused you to rest for a while until the swelling went down. Then, in your forties, you notice when the weather is cold and damp, that same injury causes you discomfort and pain. Most people would take a paracetamol for this kind of injury; most people would also be willing to go to a doctor if it affected their daily life. If, after the investigation, the doctor told you that the problem you are now experiencing is due to an injury incurred in your youth and unless you take the tablets prescribed, you will never feel better. Most people would take the meds.

Our brain is just another muscle. However, it is much more delicate than a knee or an elbow. It too can be injured and suffer damage through physical impact, but it can also be damaged by experiences, by chemical changes and by a lack of oxygen, amongst other things. It can be just as debilitating, but it is not visible.

In the past, mental health issues were associated with people being deprived of their liberties or bringing shame to their family and friends. These are archaic and outdated beliefs.

Historically, people have reported that medications used to treat mental health conditions have had unhelpful side effects. Although I am not able to say that modern medication has no side effects, since that is a matter for a professional, what I can say is that modern medications are far more advanced than they used to be. The overhaul of medication used to treat mental health over the past fifteen to twenty years has made them much safer and more appropriate for treating mental health conditions, with less likelihood of unpleasant side effects.

Nowadays, when GPs are dealing with the treatment of mental health conditions, they do not automatically prescribe medication. There are many ways to manage mental health and it is a scenario that is much better supported by businesses, sports facilities, local authorities and the wider community. This book contains ways for you to find help with your mental health which do not rely on medication alone. Hopefully, they will provide insight into alternative solutions which will help you on a journey of mental health management.

The power of one

When I was a kid, I was always very passionate about nature. As I developed, I became increasingly aware of the damage being done to the planet by human activity. In my little idealistic head, I thought I would grow up and be able to put a stop to the damage occurring on a global scale. As I grew older, I learnt it was not possible for one person to put everything right. Not even if you found yourself in an extremely powerful situation, like being the head of a major state or country. In response to this, I decided to study Environmental Science in college and university and I have gone on to enjoy a career in this field, although I had a bumpy start – more about that in future chapters.

I began working in a job where I couldn't change the entire world, but I could work with the people around me to make changes to my world and help them change theirs. As this pattern continues, it has an impact and there can be change. If we were all to adopt this approach, it would ultimately make a significant difference to the world.

I have since found out that there is something which is referred to as the Power of One.

The Power of One is not about looking after number one; it is about recognising the positive influence we as individuals can have on others. We can choose to be the positive impact and agent of change on those around us. I have seen, firsthand, the power and possibilities of this approach and I have adopted it in everything I do. I would love to do this with you in relation to mental health. Together, we can start a ripple effect, encouraging others to do the same.

Chapter 2

"Mental health is for flaky people, isn't it?"

My mate Bob

Recently, during a difficult period in his life, my friend (let's call him Bob) told me he had never given much credence to the stories he heard about people struggling with their mental health. He thought 'mental illness' was a modern description of weakness for people who were 'flaky.'

That was until lockdown.

My friend is a very accomplished blacksmith and he is as big as a grizzly bear. He is a very social person, at work and in life, he always has been. His network of friends and contacts is unbelievable. He is the type of person who, if you need a ¾ inch widget for your 40mm google-blaster, he will know where to get one, how to fit it and when you will need another.

He told me that when lockdown hit, it completely rocked his entire world. He needed to be outside and able to communicate with other people, yet overnight, the pandemic snatched those things away. The COVID-19 scenario dragged on for weeks, then months. This began to take its toll on his mental health. He was frustrated, he was bored and he was lonely and disconnected from the people he cared about. He realised the value of positive mental health and how very damaging negative mental health can be. Mental health is as important as physical health.

I have spoken with Bob several times since things returned to normal. He has acknowledged that his stubborn refusal to be open-minded to things he didn't understand and which he believed to be weaknesses, is a thing of the past for him. He also told me he is more supportive and open-minded about other people's frailties because of his experience during lockdown.

During the process of writing 'The Pie Eating Man's Guide to a Healthy Mind' I have been shocked by how many friends, family and colleagues have shared sad and tragic stories about how mental health has affected them and their families.

This has proven to be added motivation to get the book written and made available as soon as possible. The sooner it is available, the sooner it might assist one more person to find help.

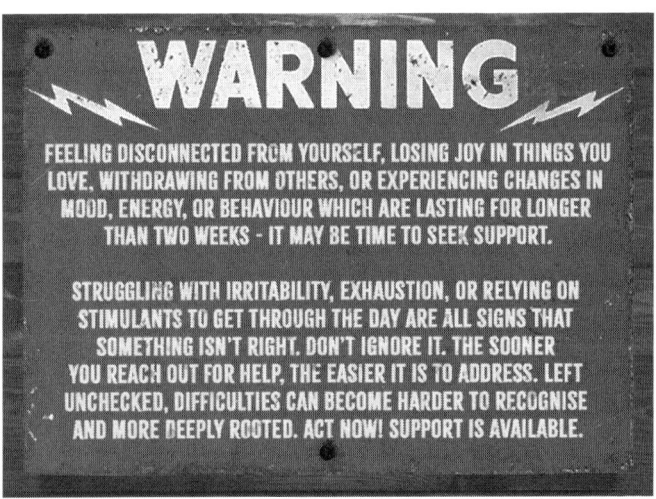

Another thing that comes up again and again in

conversation is how hard it is to know when someone needs help. Throughout this book, you will find reminders of signs to watch out for both in yourself and others.

Toxic masculinity

Toxic masculinity is the abuse of privileges given to men after centuries of societal preference and control. It focuses on the more controlling and destructive aspects of masculinity and is predominantly recognised as a way of oppressing women and femininity in society.

Traditionally, people refer to toxic masculinity as a behavioural trait driven by men, which has a negative impact on women.

I need to be very clear; the effects of toxic masculinity are very harmful and affect many people. In no way am I making light of that. However, in this section of the book, I am concentrating on the element of toxic masculinity, also driven by men, but which has a negative impact on other men.

People often overlook this element of Toxic Masculinity, yet it has an enormous impact and it is part of the reason this destructive element of societal norms continues.

One in eight men are reported to have an anxiety or stress disorder. It is believed that the true figures are more likely to be much higher but many people do not speak up about their issues. They fear the repercussions of making themselves look weak or shaming themselves and those around them. We simply must change this way of thinking. Let's take a look at some of the behaviours traditionally associated with Toxic Masculinity:

- An expectation and driver for power and physical and sexual domination over others.
- The requirement to overlook and devalue women's opinions, bodies and sense of self.

- An expectation that men should have no need to ask for help and that they should need no financial, emotional or practical support.
- The repression of emotions other than anger and competitiveness.
- An expectation that any display of behaviours which have in the past been perceived as 'feminine' is a flaw and should be shunned.
- Judging any form of non-traditional 'masculine' behaviour as shameful and weak.
- Equating any form of affection for another man as sexual attraction and calling it out.
- Creating an outcast of men who do not fit the perceived 'masculine' mould.

These toxic values impact how we put our health and our lives at risk because they have caused us to believe that seeking help or being unwell is not 'manly'. We may be ostracised by those around us if we fail to consider this.

The ridiculous thing is that most people have or will suffer with their mental health at some point in their lives. If we do not have personal experience of this, we will know someone who does and if they are anything like me, they will not seek help because they think that someone will judge them.

Toxic Masculinity is one of the biggest negative drivers in society for both men and women. It causes people to concentrate their aims in competing to be the 'haves' as opposed to the 'have nots'.

It is where I see some of the darkest effects of social media, advertising and the press polluting lifestyles. The pressure upon individuals to enter into the continuous comparison of lifestyles and 'success' based on wealth and luxury is destructive. Provided that we have the finances enough to be safe and comfortable, true contentment is found in family, friends, love, nature, mindfulness and self-management.

The suppression of emotions, particularly in men, often occurs from a young age. The use of phrases such as 'man up' or 'don't be a girl' from role models and peers can leave many men afraid or even unable to recognise and speak about how they feel. Men often become emotionally constipated and are much more likely to take to alcohol or substance abuse. It can also lead them to become irritable, spending or gambling excessively and even show bullying characteristics.

Suicide is the biggest killer of both men and women under the age of fifty. Four out of five of those suicides will be men. Men who kill themselves are more likely to be from a lower socio-economic background and often work in unskilled jobs. It is in these arenas where toxic masculinity thrives.

Does toxic masculinity breed more toxic masculinity?

The short answer to this question is yes. Toxic masculinity 'eats itself'; the existence of toxic masculinity and its effect on some men is cyclical and perpetuates more toxic masculinity.

The abuse of men by other men through peer pressure and 'locker room' mentality, forces those with differing opinions to remain silent. It perpetuates the negative perception of mental health issues and condemns the freedom to love outside of peer norms. This is a significant factor contributing to the negative associations with mental health issues in men.

It takes a brave voice to oppose these groups, but we need to talk about these subjects more. It should be possible to create safe spaces for like-minded people to come together to talk and gain confidence. We need to do it in safe and cohesive environments that allow lessons to be learned and acted upon.

Don't just stand there

If you find yourself as a bystander to a situation don't just turn a blind eye and walk on. If we have any chance of changing things for the better we all need to actively step up and do something to help. In scenarios when someone is being treated in a way that is unacceptable, bystanders are often reluctant to get involved for fear of being hurt; fear of being made a victim themselves; or simply because they don't want to stand out.

Have you ever been with a group of people who are laughing at you or saying cruel things to you, things that hurt but you simply put up with? You assume it would go away, but it carries on and on and there is nothing you can do to make it stop. You know that if you say something now, it will just make things worse.

Most times, these things do go away, but while they are happening, they can be all-consuming for the victim; at work and at home. It is a very lonely and helpless place to be.

Sometimes it takes that one bystander to step in and do something to help. I am sad to say that I have been the victim, the reluctant bystander and sadly, the person making someone feel bad, even if it was not intentional.

I am pleased to say however, that the position I have been in the most is the person who helped. I helped people at school who were having a hard time through no fault of their own. I help people at work and it is not uncommon for me to protect a stranger in the street too.

Ninety percent of the time, people just need to be reminded that their actions are unacceptable and the situation is something that has gone too far. Most good-hearted people would want to know if their actions were causing someone issues, so that they can stop.

There is caution to be had though, there is no point in two people being hurt, so it is important that you choose the correct way to help.

Being a 'good Samaritan' does not always mean 'getting into the thick of it'. You do not need to be part of the scenario directly, but you might be the person who speaks to a senior member of staff, a police officer, a parent or someone who has influence over the situation to help the person who is coming to harm.

It is important that we all come together to oppose these negative behaviours and step in when they get out of hand. We must become more thoughtful and supportive of one another to encourage wellness.

Society has changed and it is OK for you to change too. It can feel hypocritical to step in to stop a scenario, which in the past we could have been part of – for the wrong reasons. This feeling of discomfort is the reason we should not just let it happen, because it means we know it is wrong.

Trust me, changing your view on something because you have learned it was wrong, does not make you a hypocrite. It makes you a good and wise person.

THESE BEHAVIOURS CAUSE PEOPLE TO END THEIR LIVES AND IT IS NOT OK.

WHEN THINGS GO TOO FAR,

IT IS NOT BANTER;

IT IS NOT FUN; OR LEG PULLING.

How can we help people?

It is healthy to recognise the impact of toxic masculinity on society as a whole.

Treating people fairly with kindness and respect, no matter their age, gender, sexuality, race or religion, is the way forward.

Those of us who are seen as being in a position of influence should be seeking to oppose toxic masculinity and helping people to feel valued, worthy and safe. The more worthy and safe a person feels, the more likely they will function to their best ability. This is particularly important in the workplace and in educational environments.

If nothing changes, it will remain the same

Men with mental health issues often feel marginalised, or that they have nowhere to go to have 'the conversation'. Reach out to people you haven't heard from for a while and have the chat. Check that they are OK and that they know you are there if they need you.

Together we can help to stop this and help to support men in recognising the value of speaking about things.

Growing up I was always taught to stick up for people who can't stick up for themselves. When I see behaviour which is unacceptable, or if I see that the mentality within a team is toxic, I will call it out. I make a point of finding an appropriate time to speak to those who seem to be struggling and offer them support. This should be done when others are not around to avoid causing embarrassment.

If you feel you are able, be an influencer of change, someone who changes culture for the better. Things will never change, if they remain the same.

Remember, if someone says they're upset by something we've said or done, it's not really our place to decide they shouldn't be. Just because it didn't seem upsetting to us doesn't mean it wasn't to them. We don't get to choose whether or not we have caused upset. We do get to choose whether or not to apologise, and in most instances we should.

So what can we do about it?

When you see unacceptable behaviour, or if you see that the culture within a team, group of friends or in the office is toxic, do something. Speak to people who seem to be struggling and offer them support. Approach management and group leaders and ask them to speak about things in a more inclusive and sensitive manner. If you can't do these things, seek out new groups to be with who are more aligned with your way of thinking and invite others from the group to join you.

As with many of the issues discussed in this book, it's always wise to look at your 'fluid' and even your 'fixed' self and consider whether changes need to take place. It is likely to take time and it will not always be comfortable.

Chapter 3
My childhood

Growing up a bit broken

As I have already mentioned, I'm a normal bloke. I grew up in the eighties in a working-class household and my brother and I were predominantly raised by our mum. She did an amazing job.

What I mean by she did an 'amazing job' is that she had it tough. She had very little money and we must have been exhausting to raise (particularly me). Despite this, we have reaped the benefits of a happy childhood filled with love, healthy meals, laughter with friends and everything we needed to thrive.

Now, this doesn't mean that we are both super successful millionaires. We are both regular guys, with regular jobs and regular family lives. But that's exactly what success looks like to me.

I was extremely hard work until I was around twelve years old. But it wasn't until I was in my thirties that I realised there might be a reason for this. I genuinely think that I have been depressed for as long as I can remember. Eventually, I was diagnosed with ADHD.

When I was a child, they called me 'hyperactive'. If I ate a sweet, had an ice-cream, or drank a drink more colourful than a Weetabix, I turned into a Tasmanian Devil crossed with a Honey badger (see glossary for details).

Growing up, my depression and hyperactivity manifested itself in frustration, which became anger with defiant and destructive behaviour. I could destroy a family party in a heartbeat. I had no qualms about refusing to get in the car, walking ten miles home rather than concede defeat and take a lift.

Even now I still remember how it felt to have that frustration running through my veins; like electrically charged poison. My anger led me to imagine smashing up everything in my room. Thankfully, I never went to that extreme; I broke some things, but not the whole room. Instead, I would destroy things that were dear to me, like certificates or pictures and posters I loved.

My belief was that this behaviour would get me heard; instead, it broke my heart when the red mist cleared and I had to pick up the pieces from my overreaction, both literally and metaphorically.

My mum did her best to tire me out; I swam a lot and I was always playing out with friends, but that was not enough. Sometimes when I knew I had anger or frustration rising in me, my mum would put up her hands and let me punch them, trying to help me release some of that frustration. Just behind that anger were painful tears and a lump in my throat. She could see the pain in my eyes. She understood, but could do little to help.

Even as I am writing this, I can feel it again. My arms are fizzing and my fingers and toes are clenching. I would strike out at my mum, my friends, my teachers and my family, including my brother (who, to be fair, did like to taunt me so I am only 50 percent sorry for that).

When friends told their parents that I was visiting, I imagined them rolling their eyes and hiding their best china. Despite all of that and mainly because of the excellent work my mum had put in, I believe I was quite a nice kid, with good manners when I visited people's homes. I believe most of my friends' parents saw the good in me.

I loved visiting friends because they had dads and dads to me were something I desperately wished I had more access to. If a 'dad' ever suggested play fighting, or asked for help with DIY, or with digging the garden, I was always first in the queue to help. I unofficially adopted all my best friends' parents and to this day I love them all dearly.

The legacy of being a little s**t!

Being a handful as a kid creates a problem; people never forget. They remember the bad behaviour, rather than all the good stuff you did. Having been such a destructive force growing up, with no fear of causing damage towards things and people I loved, meant that even when I grew out of it, it was often the subject of discussion at the family events and parties. My family regularly reminded me of all the upset and disruption I had caused and no amount of apologising for my actions seemed to stop them from raising this issue, which is not good for a teenager's mental health.

Being uncomfortable with the child I had been and the damage I had caused to people I cared so much about; to be reminded of the things I did, as part of family jokes at every event I attended and on every family holiday really stung. I was sorry; I had changed, but it was like someone repeatedly snapping an elastic band on the end of my nose, but not allowing me to let my eyes water. It ached and it ached bad.

Boredom is underrated

When I was younger, before we all had a mobile phone to fill our time, I used to sit and think. Some people called it boredom, but I don't remember feeling bored as a kid. When your parents went into a shop and left you in the car, or on days in the holidays when no friends were available to play out, these were the times that our brains had to fill the gaps. We would have to find alternative things to do.

Sitting there, my imagination would run wild about future jobs, hobbies and things I would like to achieve. It was also when I would actively notice the world around me, the leaves on the trees outside, the funny spots on the ceiling of the car that would make my eyes go funny, how the seat belts worked. Nowadays, we are all encouraged to sit still, thinking or observing nature. And we call it mindfulness.

We had a computer, a 'Sinclair ZX Spectrum 48k' no less! Back then, you did not just switch your machine on and start playing games. If you wanted to play a game, you had to insert a cassette…and wait. This could take fifteen mins or more, giving us more time to sit and think.

Again, my mind would get to work imagining. Or I would use the time actively playing with my Star Wars figures or transformers. Using these toys required me to create my own stories; figuring out how to build a structure for the figures to stand on or swing from, playing with them in the bath, imagining that they were scuba diving or something else equally exciting.

We lived on a close with no through traffic, so it was safe to play out in the street. Our street 'gang' was called the 'Rokeby Riders,' and we were always buzzing around on our bikes. We played in nearby fields and in each other's gardens, building shelters and dens from sticks, leaves and grass. We learned about physics without even realising it, because if we did not build those shelters well, they would collapse.

Ponds filled with tadpoles, frogs and sticklebacks surrounded the fields around us. My best friend and neighbour in those days was a girl called Alison. We spent a lot of time together and were always up to something. Most local people thought we were brother and sister. We were always catching things and putting them in a jar to have a look at; we always had a collection of snails living off nettles in a tub and Alison had an old bath in her garden, where we watched up close as tadpoles transformed into frogs.

It's a bit of a cliché, but we would be out from dawn till dusk. Only coming back for lunch or a drink and that was only if we could not take a pack-up with us.

Those days with Alison were some of the best days of my life. We once tried to dig all the way to Australia, but after a centimetre or two, it became obvious that the hardness of the ground meant it was going to take some time. Instead, we decided to dig our own graves, but that was also quite hard work, so we went indoors to play a board game instead.

What I am trying to say is that things are not like that anymore for any age group. Most people have almost no downtime in their lives. With a mobile phone in your hand, there is no need to use your imagination. You can fill those rare unoccupied moments scrolling through social media or watching online videos created by someone else.

We didn't have kids' TV available twenty four hours a day. Our TV had four channels and we had to wait for movies and TV series to air when the channels decided.

We spent our time in friendship groups, laughing and joking with our mates all day and looking out for each other.

We filled the hours with our thoughts and plans for our future; spent hours studying the artwork inside an album cover, listening to the album in the order intended by the artist. We would make mistakes in our heads without having to make them for real and we would overcome problems without having to invest in the failures.

Thinking time was invaluable to me; and it is something I still carve out time for. It feeds my abilities as a lateral thinker and helps me take on creative projects successfully. It has made me an excellent communicator and networker. In fact, I would say that networking is my first superpower. My second superpower is my ADHD, but I will get into that later.

Senior school

When I turned twelve and started senior school, much of my frustration and anger seemed to fade. I was far happier, surrounded by a good group of friends and felt that my teachers treated me with a lot more respect. I was still eager to be the class clown and had a tendency to talk too much, but I like to think my energy was mostly positive.

I went to a big school with around a hundred and twenty five teachers in total. I reckon that at least ninety percent of them taught me at one time or another and every single teacher who ever taught me sent me out of class for a cocky comment, or for talking too much. Weirdly though, I don't think many of them truly disliked me.

Despite this, I loved senior school and I had some fabulous teachers including Mrs Harman, Mr Skoyles, Miss Thorpe, Mr Salter, Mr Scott and Mr Cork. They 'got' me, helped me and made me a better person. I didn't always see eye to eye with some of them at first, but it turned out that this was because they wanted the best for me and they could see that I was not achieving my full potential. I now believe that without the active intervention and care shown by some of these teachers, I could have been on a path to self-destruction. I had the potential to go either way. Even now, although much more watered down, I believe that alternative path could still be available to me. I think this is why I try hard not to judge people. Who knows what is around the corner? Just one stroke of bad luck could change everything for any of us.

Chapter 4

The 'B' word

(Remarkably similar to the 'OG' Jesus Sandals)

Jesus sandals

The earliest memory I have of being bullied was at school, when I was around seven or eight years old. As I said before, we did not have a great deal of money in our house, but mum always tried to ensure that we had decent leather footwear for school. Like most families back then, we bought our shoes from Clarks' shoe shop.

I had unusually wide feet (obviously, I still have the same pair of feet and they are still extremely wide!). This meant that the choice of shoes available to me was always limited. Inevitably, I would end up with brown leather shoes with one or two buckles on them. They were not exactly the height of fashion.

There were some nasty kids at my school who remained horrible until they left. I remember them crowding round me and calling me Jesus Sandals and it hurt. It really hurt. Not least because I knew it would be this way for months, as I only got new shoes when I grew out of the old ones. Even worse than that, though, was that I knew I would end up with similar shoes every time!

When you know your mum is doing her best and are aware that everything else is more expensive, you have no choice but to go along with it.

When incidents like this happened, I had to make a choice. Do I shrivel away and become a quiet victim, or do I stand up for myself and become as loud as they were unpleasant? I chose the latter. I worked out that bullies are sly; they waited until other people could not hear, or for when teachers and dinner ladies were not around to tell them off. I also figured out that the louder I was, the less likely they were to attack me. Also, if I 'owned' the things they saw as my frailties, they could not use them to attack me.

Nowadays I often introduce myself as the chubby ginger fella with a big beard. When I did that back then, it meant that there were less loose threads for the bad guys to pull on to unravel me.

The other coping mechanism I developed was humour; the ability to laugh at myself and to take the micky out of people at a level that is entertaining and not bullying. This kept most bullies at bay.

All of this helped, but I still got involved in my fair share of scrapes when these tactics failed.

These experiences taught me it is possible for us to compartmentalise how people behave towards us. This does not necessarily mean that the perpetrator will stop mistreating us, but it may minimise the effects of their behaviour on us, until we find ourselves in a position to change the situation.

As I have grown older I have learned that most bullies have had difficulties in their own lives and their way of managing them is to lash out at others. This obviously does not make it right, but now I am an adult looking back at some of the instances of bullying I experienced, I can see that the bullies may have had unpleasant lives and they were envious of my positive and outgoing demeanour.

What is bullying?

Determining the difference between what is considered appropriate behaviour; 'leg pulling', 'banter', 'sarcasm' or 'taking the p*$$' and inappropriate behaviour; bullying and harassment can be challenging.

Here in the UK, a lot of comedy is based on irony. This can be challenging for some people. Something said in jest may be horribly offensive to one person but could equally be completely hilarious to someone else! Knowing the people, you are dealing with and doing your best to avoid subjects they are sensitive about is always wise.

The definition of bullying

Although I cannot find a specific legal definition of bullying, bullying in the workplace occurs when a person regularly mistreats someone while they are at work or when a person is mistreated by someone they work with. Here are some examples of behaviours that may lead to bullying.

- Constant criticism both verbally and by email/messages
- The spreading of malicious rumours
- Personal attacks, both physical and verbal
- Belittling and humiliation
- Exclusion and ostracism of people from groups, training or even conversations
- Unfair treatment
- Regularly undermining someone

- People making demands of you outside of works time and/or contacting you by phone, text or email, regularly outside of work

This list is not exhaustive. There are many other examples of bullying behaviour.

It is essential that if you feel you are experiencing bullying, you should investigate the behaviours and determine whether they are actually bullying or are you being over sensitive to reasonable behaviour?

Protected characteristics

It is important to note that bullying as a stand-alone behaviour is not illegal. However, most organisations who employ staff will have a bullying and harassment policy that they expect their staff to adhere to.

It is the responsibility of all organisations to ensure that their workplace is safe for their staff and that, in the event of a problem, they will take all reasonable steps to protect the wellbeing of their employees. This policy should include steps for protecting mental health, as well as physical health.

Harassment, which can form part of a bullying case, is unlawful under the Equality Act 2010. This applies when the unwanted behaviour relates to one or more of the following protected characteristics:

- age
- sex
- disability
- gender reassignment
- marriage and civil partnership
- pregnancy and maternity

- race
- religion or belief
- sexual orientation

It is important for you to know that the law has recognised these characteristics to protect people from harassment.

Over the past fifty years, the perceptions of many of these protected characteristics have changed. Lots of people still find it difficult to understand what the changes are and they can be unaware of which phrases and descriptive terms are acceptable. I believe it is OK to make mistakes; however, once we are made aware of our error, it is important to apologise and we should attempt to use the correct terms from then on.

Similarly, if someone innocently uses a phrase or term that is unacceptable, we have a responsibility to explain politely that the phrase is no longer acceptable. We live in a world where people are quick to anger and to take offence. But it is also a world where people believe they can say what they like; because they have always used a certain phrase, or because we have 'freedom of speech'.

While there may be an element of truth in this, we all have a responsibility; to be kind to people and avoid causing upset. We should always do our best to avoid causing offence to someone, but we should also try to avoid taking offence because of someone's behaviour. If we live this way and we are prepared to share the benefit of our knowledge and experience to help others understand, the world would be a far better place.

Am I a bully?

A bully does not have to be someone in charge. Bullies can appear in any role. Similarly, we can be the victim of bullying, no matter what role we find ourselves in.

Sometimes, people who bully are oblivious to their behaviour. It is important to exercise caution and mindfulness when dealing with individuals we suspect may be bullying us. Accusing someone of being a bully, when they are unaware that their actions could be construed as bullying and can be very upsetting. Often, the instant response is for them to argue or defend themselves.

If someone accuses you of bullying behaviour, the best way to deal with it is to sit down with them and discover what is making them feel that way; ask them for examples of behaviour that they felt was unacceptable. Once you are fully informed, you can discuss the possibility of taking time to think about the matters discussed and coming back to them with a way forward. You could also apologise there and then and advise that you were not aware that your actions had been causing upset and that you will work with them to change these behaviours.

I appreciate that this all seems a little 'fairytale,' but imagine if we all took more time to talk about these things constructively; to find better ways of working together. These are the best solutions to such issues.

I am a big guy and come across as confident and loud, which means I may seem potentially intimidating when you first meet me. The problem is, I do not really recognise how big I am, and I am a genuinely enthusiastic person, particularly when meeting new people. My wife tells me that this combination can come across as a little threatening, especially to people who are not naturally as loud or as big as me.

Once people get to know me, I am happy to say they usually realise that this view of me is incorrect and see that I am a big softy. But I can see how I can seem a bit like a friendly Rottweiler playing with a kitten, or depending on your point of view, an aggressive Rottweiler about to eat a kitten!

In my case I am allergic to cats and the kitten is way more likely to come out on top, if indeed I am the rottweiler, which I try not to be.

How can bullying impact on individuals?

When I encountered bullying in my horrible job, it seemed to be because the bully felt threatened by me and they had to 'put me in my place'; because I had a degree and they didn't, and because I had a happy home life and they may not have. The impact of bullying on people like you and me can be far-reaching and extremely disruptive. Most people have experienced some sort of bullying in their lives. It may have been short term and had a limited impact, or it might have had a more serious effect.

This book does not really aim to address childhood issues, but it is important to recognise that most people experience bullying for the first time in their childhood and this can make their lives thoroughly miserable.

Bullying in adulthood can function as a trigger for increased stress, anxiety and depression. Equally, some behaviours which may not be bullying on their own could trigger people if they formed part of a bullying situation when they were young. It is important that if we are feeling this way; we explain and ask the perpetrator to be aware of this.

When we have our first experience of bullying as an adult, it can be very disturbing. It may not feel like it at the time, but when we are children there is a level of protection available from the adults in our life. When we are grownups, that support is not available to us in the same way, which can leave us feeling very lonely and exposed.

Being bullied leaves us feeling undermined, resentful and in a mess, with no control over our home and work lives. It causes us to experience many of the symptoms associated with anxiety, stress, depression and other mental health conditions.

My experience of bullying at work left me mentally scarred. Even now, certain circumstances take me straight back to that time. It's a form of Post Traumatic Stress Disorder (PTSD). I refer to them as triggers. It might be a scenario that arises, or a phrase that is used, and it fires me back into that dark place.

If I've learned one thing from being bullied, it was the value of somebody else seeing it and offering support; particularly if that person is prepared to be a witness and confirm what they saw.

If you find yourself in the position where you can support someone who is being bullied, please do, as it is a very lonely and dark place to be on your own.

Dealing with bullies

One thing I would like to remind you, the reader, is that bullies tend to be bullies because of their own insecurities. They project traits they dislike in themselves onto others, masking their struggles behind cruelty or intimidation. Remembering this can help you take their words and actions less personally.

Bullying is often a sign of jealousy or dissatisfaction within the bully's own life. The problem usually lies with them, not you. Knowing this doesn't necessarily make things easier, but understanding it can be a step toward not letting their behaviour define how you see yourself.

Guidance for people being bullied in the workplace

Just because something is not illegal does not mean that there is no protection in place. Employers need to take their role in this seriously, but accusations of bullying can be very inconvenient and not all employers deal with them as they should.

If you believe you are being bullied in the workplace, I encourage you to go through the following steps:

First, it is important to consider whether you are a victim of bullying and harassment. Start by checking the company policy. This is important for several reasons. Bullying and harassment accusations must be evidenced for them to be taken seriously by your employer, your union and/or your legal representatives.

You will need to provide proper examples of the behaviours you believe to be bullying. Remember, bullying and harassment cases can be very upsetting and destructive to one, both, or all those involved. Always explore whether it is possible to resolve the issue before things become too uncomfortable. For instance, consider speaking to the person involved and let them know how their behaviour makes you feel and let them know it is unacceptable.

It is always worth considering putting your concerns in writing to the people responsible, so that you can keep copies and have evidence of exactly what was said. If the person/people responsible are not your manager, it is important to share your concerns with your manager as well, to see what their thoughts on the scenarios are. There may be something they can do to help. By arranging a meeting with your manager present as an official representative to both parties, you can discuss the issues properly and professionally.

The disruption caused by a bullying claim can be colossal; another reason it is important to make sure that your concerns are accurate. I managed my claim poorly because I didn't know any better and the organisation handled it poorly too; they should have known better but were probably covering their arse! The fallout from my situation was devastating for me, for my future with the organisation and for my 'relationship' with the person who I had made the accusation to.

Remember, the person you are accusing may not even realise they are being cruel; it could be a simple misunderstanding between you and them. The damage that a bullying claim can do to a person's career, whether it is true or false, is extensive. You must be confident that what you are experiencing is bullying before you take official action.

Feeling bullied or harassed? What should you do?

When I was being bullied, I spoke to the people I worked with who I trusted enough to ask if they felt I was being treated fairly? I tried to do this without being too obvious, I made sure I did it when my boss was not there. Once I had established that there were several occasions when they felt the way I was being treated was not fair and that I was being treated differently than they were, I raised my concerns.

This was a mistake, there were other steps I should have taken first. If I had done that, I might have had a better portfolio of evidence to show the issues I had faced. This is even more important when you consider I was not in a good or organised state of mind. I did not recall or document events accurately. Which meant it was difficult to plead my case, particularly when standing up against someone who was not experiencing the effects of bullying and was superior to me within the organisation. If you believe you are being bullied, my advice is:

Keep a diary of events which you believe are unacceptable - Make notes as soon after the incident as possible; try to describe them in full, including the reasons that you feel what happened was wrong. Make a note of witnesses, the date and time and how you responded.

Gauge the opinions of people around you that you trust - They can help you understand whether you might be oversensitive, or if there are other things occurring that you are not aware of. It is important to hear all those you ask and not just the messages of those you agree with.

Join a trade union - They have lots of powers and access to legal information that can be extremely useful. A trade union will only support you in a grievance if you have been a member since before the time you make the accusation.

Maintaining relationships - You should always attempt to sort the problem out informally if you can. Depending on the situation, this might be easier said than done. If you are raising concerns about a colleague or someone who is not your direct manager, this is always the best option. Make a note of this in your diary too, along with any outcome.

If issues continue after you have sought support from these groups, you may wish to seek legal advice from your Union, your HR department, a legal expert, a senior colleague you trust and/or an organisation like ACAS (Advisory, Conciliation and Arbitration Service) using their helpline for advice - See the 'Helpful resources' section at the end of the book for more information on this service.

Be the difference

It is over twenty years since I was bullied at work. Although it was exceedingly difficult at the time and made me very unwell, I got through it. If I had been offered better advice at the time and I had been more organised, I don't think things would have gone as badly for me. if I had been given more support by on-lookers I would have felt stronger and in a better position to do something about it.

If you ever find yourself in this scenario, I assure you that things will improve. It doesn't always help to hear this at the time and it is a cliché, but time is truly the greatest healer. If you see someone else in this scenario and if you can, please be the person who steps in and offers support. It really does make a difference to know that you are not alone.

Take proper advice and be organised, don't ever lose belief in yourself as you can go on to be successful and lead a happy life. Who knows? You may even go on to write a book one day!

Chapter 5

My mental health

Breakdowns and change

An old friend of mine, Barty (yes Barty you are both old and you have been my friend for nearly thirty years) once told me that during our lives we go through experiences and when you look back, you can almost put your finger on the day you saw your life change forever. There are likely to be several instances like this during your life and they are very important. He was right.

For the record, Barty was also the person who told me, 'If you are going to tell a story, you need to tell the WHOLE story from the very beginning and you must include all the interesting details.' So, he is the person you can blame for the drivel you are currently wading through!

Fixed and Fluid self

Over the years, I have attended some excellent leadership courses.

The courses which have benefitted me most have seen participants being asked to analyse themselves and their personality traits. Some of them are scarily accurate.

What I have found is that we seem to have two main sections to our personalities and behaviours. We have a 'Fixed self' and a 'Fluid self'.

Fixed self

As the names suggest, the fixed self is very rigid, although that can change with practice. In the same way that a stiff, unused muscle sometimes needs warming up and working on before it can be manipulated successfully.

Our fluid self, however, is far easier to manipulate and change and may reflect the scenario we find ourselves in.

The fixed self is the part of us that is inherently rigid, with fixed feelings. These encompass many core beliefs often embedded in us during our early lives as part of a job or role we have held (e.g., being a parent) for a long period of our lives. It also relates to our personality traits such as stubbornness, kindness, jealousy and selflessness.

They relate to our thoughts on things we find to be intrinsically right or wrong; things we find totally unacceptable, like racism, abuse, or a robbery. The things that people might say or do when in your company, that you would speak up about instinctively to support or oppose.

Although our fixed self is often relatively fixed, impactful experiences might change that. They might also change over time, through education, or peer alignment, or when in a particular job.

Fluid self

Our fluid self is the part of us that is more adaptable and open to change. We may find we are less concerned about the outcome of a situation or more comfortable making different decisions based on the context of the day. We might be able to see both sides of an argument.

I often imagine it to be like a fruit like a peach or avocado. In the centre they have a hard stone which would be the fixed self and the softer outer flesh the fluid self.

Within both our fixed and fluid selves there are traits which we will be more and less comfortable with. What is important is our awareness of them.

The value of other people's views on you

You may have heard of a 360° review, they are commonly used in the workplace and can be valuable in personal growth. It involves gathering anonymous feedback from a mix of people around you — seniors, peers, and juniors — who answer a set of questions about how you handle different situations. The aim is to give a well-rounded view of your strengths and areas for improvement.

The purpose of the 360° feedback system is to help someone see elements of their personality which they may otherwise be blind to.

These blind spots are often the most useful behaviours to be aware of. They serve as an excellent foundation to learn about areas of our personalities which would otherwise remain hidden. Once we are aware of them, we can nourish the most wholesome parts and manage the parts which we feel are less beneficial to us. There may also be aspects of our personalities that are unhelpful to our mental state. Once we are aware, we can deal with them.

To show why this is useful, during the writing of this book I started by simply spewing my thoughts onto the page. Once that was done, I read over it and added, deleted, or adjusted things I had written. Then I sent a copy of the transcript to Penny, my editor. Penny goes through my work and makes it flow better.

What I have found is that I use the following phrases way too much when I am writing: "I think", "actually" and "is that" to name but a handful. These phrases are not wrong and it is not wrong to use them, but I have overused them making the original drafts of the book 'clunky' and harder to read. The good thing about knowing this 'is that' 'I think' that I 'actually' use them less now ☺.

We can do the same with our fixed and fluid selves when we are better informed.

It is important to note that some aspects of our personalities, the ones which we are less comfortable with, such as aggression and insistence, can still be an advantage when well managed and controlled. They have overlapping links with determination and will, so don't be too hasty to manage them out of your personality.

A change is as good as a rest – Life pivots

As far as life changing events go, I can think of several specific events in my life that really stick out. It is useful to know when these 'life pivots' occur and to know that it is possible to influence them if you feel you need to. These life pivots can cause some of the most rapid changes to our fixed selves that we experience in our lifetimes, which is why they are so memorable and important. They actually shape our personalities, our values and the things we hold dear.

My Life Pivots		
Description of life pivot	When it happened?	How things changed
My first trip abroad	7 yrs old	My eyes were opened to travel
Starting senior school	12 yrs old	I felt much happier day 2 day

A blank version of this form is available for your use in Chapter 25.

My first trip abroad

The first pivot in my life was the first time I went abroad. As I mentioned before, there was not a lot of money around as I was growing up, but when I was seven, my mum's partner kindly offered to take us all to the Middle East. I was so excited! I saved £11 in my money box to take with me for spending money and for Christmas (we went in July) I got a Lilo with a window in it to allow me to see what was going on below me in the sea.

When we finally visited, the experience blew my mind. We landed at a military airport, which was extremely exciting for a young boy. I will never forget that feeling, disembarking from the air-conditioned 'Air2000' plane in the dark and walking through the curtain of intense desert heat. We stayed in a small tourist town on the Red Sea coast. Little did I know back then how important that visit to the Red Sea would be in the shaping of my future.

Being blessed with an excellent memory, I could probably fill an entire chapter, if not a book, on the wonderful experiences I had on this holiday. Falling in love with the experience of travelling abroad, with the differences between people, with language, with heat, with ancient things. Seeing my first palm tree and climbing it (See Photo 5 in the photos section); playing in a swimming pool from morning to night. Seeing the largest and brightest coloured fruits I had ever seen; I saw pomegranates growing on a tree! Then there were the antiquities and historical wonders that I had only ever heard of in books. And I set my first hotel toaster with the weird rotating grill of doom inside on fire.

Most breathtaking of all was being introduced to the wonder of The Red Sea. I fell in love with marine life. This is how I describe it when I talk about the Red Sea to people who have never experienced it:

I remember watching the film Oliver Twist. At the end, Fagin runs across a rickety wooden bridge over a muddy waterway, with a treasure chest under his arm. As he runs, he stumbles, dropping the treasure chest. It falls into the soggy mud, where it opens. Inside, the chest is full of treasure; the sort of treasure that, as a child, you imagined filled Aladdin's cave. Gold and great big jewels of all colours and shapes (I was so engrossed in the film, according to my mum, when the chest fell, I instinctively reached out to grab it).

When I put on a snorkel and mask and looked beneath the sapphire blue waves of the Red Sea, it was as if I had opened a living version of that treasure chest. Marine life of every colour, size and shape; the most wonderful thing I had ever seen in my life. I was already passionate about wildlife, but this took things to a new level and ultimately shaped my future interests, education, career and life choices. (See Photo 6 in the photos section).

Going to Uni

I grew up on the outskirts of Hull and I loved it there. In some quarters, Hull gets a bad rap, which is very unfair. It is a great city, full of good people. I made lifelong friends there and we are all still very close. At nineteen, I had finished sixth form and my friends and I were all gearing up to disappear off to our various jobs or university courses across the country. Overall, my friends and I were nice people, but I was aware of a part of my personality that I didn't like.

We were teenagers and sarcasm was our first language. Sometimes I said things which could be cutting and cruel. Inside me I knew that leaving Sixth form, which was part of my school and going to Uni in a new town, was my opportunity to shed my skin. I could discard the part of me I didn't much like, helping me to become a better person who would treat people in a better way.

This was a decision I made and largely accomplished.

There are friends and colleagues who would shoot me down if I said that I was no longer sarcastic (it remains one of my favourite sports)! The difference now is that I try not to be cruel, furthermore I try to ensure that the humour I use does not have a 'victim'. I have no time for racism, sexism, genderism etc., and for me humour without a victim is funnier, cleverer and much more enjoyable. There is no worse feeling for me than to know that I may have hurt someone's feelings or insulted them, through me trying to have some fun with them. Still occasionally

I get it wrong, but each time it happens I am truly sorry and I always do what I can to put it right.

Breakdown #1

I was lucky enough to have what I would describe as my first and most spectacular breakdown between the ages of twenty and twenty-five. As far as breakdowns go, it was bad for me and my family, but I don't think it was as damaging as it could have been. So how can something traumatic like this be lucky?

I look at it this way because it happened when I was so young, meaning that I have been able to understand the value and importance of the things that matter from a relatively early age.

There is no doubt there were financial implications for my wife and children. But the effect it had on my personality made me the person I am today.

It came about because I was being bullied at work. The whole scenario was awful. Every morning, dreading going to work, I would be sick and leave home in tears. I would scuttle down the road, muttering to myself, desperately trying to think of a way I could get out of the job and change my situation.

I would arrive at work early to get more done. I could concentrate better without feeling like I was being preyed upon. It also meant that I could complete more of the tasks I had been assigned, to reduce the chance of being called out for my failure to meet the impossible targets that had been set. The regular gaslighting meant that self-doubt over my work became a constant, gnawing concern in the back of my mind. This ended up making everything even worse.

The boss would arrive after me and I would then spend the first hour of the day massaging their ego and asking about their family, because that seemed to be the one thing to stop them from picking on me. They were the kind of person who, if they were having a bad day, made sure that the rest of the office was going to have a bad day too. Knowingly loading me down with so much work, it was physically impossible for me to complete it all on time. Then they would systematically ask how I was getting on with each task until they found one that I had not dealt with. This gave them the reason they needed to kick my arse (proverbially not physically) in front of the rest of the office for not getting everything done.

After a while, I noticed I was itching, on the palms of my hands, my wrists, my chest, the front of my shins, the tops and the bottoms of my feet. Quickly this developed into a quite unpleasant heavy stress related dermatitis and I would itch and scratch it until it bled through my clothing. I also noticed that I was getting regular heavy nosebleeds, something I had never experienced before. One night, I woke to find my whole pillow covered in blood.

I believe both issues were directly linked to the situation I found myself in at work.

This situation went on for about a year until I finally spoke up about it at a review meeting. I explained to my manager that I felt I was being bullied and I was no longer prepared to tolerate it. This complaint led to the bosses of the organisation getting involved. By this time, I was a wreck. I was the primary breadwinner in our house; we had a mortgage and bills to pay and we were looking after our two sons, aged one and eleven years old.

I had never been involved in anything like this before, so it had not occurred to me to keep a diary of incidents or make a note of things that were said. Because I was a wreck, my ability to recall things that were said and done was virtually non-existent, which made it hard to properly evidence them.

In the end, the company found in my boss's favour, which essentially gave them free rein to pick on me as and when they liked, with no opportunity for me to complain.

Feeling I had no other option, I went out every day for my lunch, no matter what the weather. Living by the seaside in the winter meant wet, windy and cold lunch breaks. It was miserable, but it was way better than being stuck inside with them. Sometimes my partner, Esther, who is now my wife, would drive over to see me and we would go off somewhere for an hour; those days were like a ray of sunshine coming through the clouds.

When you are being bullied the worst thing is that every time something nice happens, you feel filled with dread about the bad thing coming back. I would spend the whole week living for the weekend. When 6pm on Friday arrived, I would feel euphoric, but by 7pm I would start dreading Monday morning and this feeling only grew more intense as the weekend went on.

I applied for jobs, which I knew I could do, but by the time I went for an interview I would be in such a mess that I failed to present myself well, or appeared desperate and would not get the job.

After two and a half years, I had had enough. I could not go on. During that time, house prices had rocketed and our little flat had become worth significantly more than when we had bought it, so we saw a way out. We had seen a house we liked; we had a buyer for the flat and we would have enough equity that I could leave my job and concentrate on finding something else, with a financial buffer to buy me some time.

Then, just a week before completion of the sale/purchase, our sale fell through and the whole plan collapsed around our ears. I was heartbroken and so was my wife. I could not figure out how we were ever going to get out of this hole.

Finally, I booked an appointment with my GP. I walked into her office and broke down; I explained the mess I was in and she signed me off for four weeks with stress and anxiety. It was September, right around my birthday. I was full of strange emotions; but I had decided I was going to do absolutely everything I could to ensure I never had to go back into that toxic environment. Not only were my batteries empty, but they were also faulty and could only ever reach a twenty five percent charge, even at the best of times.

Esther and I went to York to visit a food festival and I remember buying fresh figs and smoked garlic; I was not at all interested in the things I had bought; the purchasing was a distraction. I can understand why people turn to buying things when they are struggling with their mental health and how this can easily get out of control.

But I also remember feeling loved and supported by my wife. I am confident that if it were not for her and my two boys; it is highly likely that I would not be here to write this book. Other things that were going on back then remain something of a blur to me, because I was in such a mental health muddle.

With a little headspace, we eventually figured it out. Our solution is not something I would necessarily recommend. Even though a mortgage was no longer required for the new house, we managed to re-mortgage our little flat. We borrowed enough money to see us through the time I needed to find another job and escape from the horrible circumstances I found myself in.

I was so unwell that I could not be involved with the remortgaging process. Instead, Esther dealt with it all. Towards the end of September, she called me on her lunch break and said that the money had gone into our account.

I felt great relief, but also guilt, fear and anxiety.

I gave notice and I left the job that day.

Interestingly, since leaving that horrible job, I discovered my bully was struggling with some challenging problems at home, which were out of their control. I can only assume that they were unhappy with their lot in life and envied mine.

Chapter 6
A new start

The beginning of my new beginning

Around the time I was going through all of this, there were several reports in the media regarding issues relating to some mental health medication. It was being reported that in some cases it could have a negative effect on people. There was still a huge stigma attached to people suffering with their mental health.

We had a small mantelpiece in our bedroom at the flat and I placed the green and white paper prescription on the mantelpiece, deciding I would not collect the prescribed medication. I would not take the meds. I was going to use that prescription as my motivation to recover.

I know a lot more about mental health medication than I did back then. Prescriptions have radically changed over the past twenty-five years. It is important to point out that I believe that competing with that prescription in my head helped me to find some 'get up and go' which aided my path to recovery. But I believe that if I had taken my medication, I might have seen a better long-term improvement than I did.

It is important to point this out, because the first thing I would recommend to anyone who is struggling with their mental health is to pay a visit to their GP and start using the medication that they prescribe.

If it does not help, or you experience side effects that don't seem right, go back to your doctor. You can usually sort these things out.

The Ramshill

With a young family, a mortgage and no job, I was now at risk of things going horribly wrong. I had no savings, just the money from re-mortgaging the flat and that was a finite resource which would have to be paid back.

My priority was to find work, so I started applying for jobs. I still lived in the area where I had been to university. When I was a student, I worked in a pub round the corner called The Ramshill, the 'Rams' as most people referred to it. I enjoyed being a barman, so I thought I would see if they had any work. What I didn't know was that the landlord, who I had known for the past five years, had left and a new couple had taken the pub over.

One Saturday night, I went into the pub and bought a pint. Some of the staff I had worked with in the past were still behind the bar, so I asked them who the new landlord was and where I could find them. It helped a bit that as a barman I had become quite popular in there; when I went in, they would cheer and shout that I was the best barman that had ever worked there. I found this embarrassing and of course it wasn't true! But it was a very welcome massage of my desperately shriveled-up ego. I imagine it also went some way to pique the interests of the new landlord and landlady.

They were called Gill and Graham and they had relocated from Birmingham to run the pub. I saw them sitting in the corner watching a band and I went over and explained who I was, asking if there was any work available. Graham confirmed they were looking for staff and told me to come in the following day for a chat. They agreed to take me on, working six nights a week. I didn't t know it then, but this small act of kindness was the first step on my road to recovery, helping me become the person I am today.

I owe a great debt to Gill and Graham. They were precisely what I needed and it seemed to have been what they needed, too. I worked there full time for about a year and then, when I got the job I have today, I continued to work there on Sunday evenings to help with petrol money.

Gill and Graham ended up moving on after their tenure at the pub. Before they left, Gill said something to me which still resonates:

"Not many things have gone right since we took this pub on but taking you (me) and Andy the chef on were the two best things we ever did."

After two and a half years of being beaten down; being made to feel I was not good enough, I had started to believe everything being said to me. This simple sentence meant the world to me and was a major step in my recovery.

Red work

I also found a job at Currys as a shop assistant. The salon where my wife was learning to be a hairstylist had recently painted its walls green, while the signage for Currys was red. At this time, our son was around two years old and he used to refer to them as 'green work' and 'red work'.

Currys also served as an important part of my recovery. Before attending Uni, I had worked in several retail roles, so working at Currys was well within my skill set; a return to something I knew well. My earliest job was in a newsagent chain in Hull and standards there were high. I learnt a great deal from them and all my subsequent retail jobs.

The management at Currys could clearly see that I was intelligent and dependable; as always, I arrived early and completed all tasks in the manner required. They were kind to me, invested in me by training me and trusting me. I was working at Currys on either the 9am – 6pm shift or the 12pm – 8pm shift.

Once I finished my day at Currys, I would go home, have something to eat, usually nod off and an hour later I would start work at the Rams and I would work until around midnight, sometimes later over the weekend. I did this for around eight months and it was hard.

Then I saw an advert for a job in the Environmental Science field, which was what I had studied at Uni. The job was fifty-five miles away and the salary was not the best, but there was a possibility that a job could come up seventeen miles away if I went for it, so I did and I got it.

With all the help I had received from the good people I had worked with since leaving that horrible job, I had begun to value myself again. My new job became my career and I have worked my way up through the ranks from the lowest paid post.

For twenty years now, I have loved my job. It was hard for the first couple of years, with a one-hundred-and-ten-mile round trip each day, on a salary of around £14,000 but it was worth it. My wife never gave up on me. I never gave up and I will never forget the people who helped me along the way. I owe them a tremendous debt.

Despite their help, I was still not back to being the old me and even now, when I go back to the offices I first worked in I can feel the pain I had in my heart when I worked there. When you have suffered with your mental health in this way and each day is slightly better than the last, it is hard to put your finger on when you reach the point where you can say you are better. (See photos 7 and 8 in the photos section).

Only later, when you are at your best, can you go back to those places and understand the process of recovery. You may remember me mentioning when worked at the horrible job my legs, feet, hands and wrists were covered in a kind of itchy dermatitis. It was not until a holiday in Egypt in 2018, seventeen years after it started, that my right leg finally cleared up from that condition.

After the initial two years of working in the new job a vacancy came up at the other office, only seventeen miles from my home. They offered me the job and I still work there today.

Breakdown #2

There was another period in the summer of 2020, where I was teetering on the edge of another breakdown. But I recognised the signs and smashed my emotional gear box into reverse to stop me rolling down the hill, as I knew my brakes were dodgy. In the first week of lockdown I caught COVID-19 and I have never been so ill. There was so much going on at the time and in the weeks and months that followed. Just having the illness was stressful, aside from everything else that was happening.

We were the first people we knew of to get the illness in our town and we felt a huge obligation not to pass it on. It felt a little like we had the plague. Nobody went out. We followed the guidelines and we looked after each other. If times had been different, I would have gone into hospital; I was so unwell. I experienced coughing fits which lasted for forty five minutes and left me gasping for breath. Everybody we heard about who went into the hospital was dying. Also, we knew the hospitals did not have the manpower or the safety equipment needed to deal with it, so I did not want to go.

There were no testing kits and you couldn't get an appointment with a GP, so we just did our best. At this time, we were getting mixed messages from our government, in our homes and in our workplaces. I was trying to lead a team of frontline essential workers at work and keep their morale up which was difficult, to say the least. I could see lots of people not adhering to the rules and working when they shouldn't be; accepting large payouts of cash that they were not entitled to and it felt unfair. All these things cranked up my stress levels and I started feeling ill again.

I have learned that I am triggered and find things very difficult when there are confusing and conflicting messages being issued. It is likely that this is a carry-over from when I was in the horrible job, but I seem to remember feeling this way as a child too.

At first I didn't realise, that I had become weighed down; I felt close to tears a lot of the time and the more conflicting information I was exposed to, the worse it got.

At this time, I decided I should take my own advice and seek medical support for my mental health.

Unfortunately we were in the first spring/summer of the pandemic. People were being asked not attend the GP and to be honest, I had been so ill with Covid, I really didn't want to catch it again. So, I emailed them explaining my feelings and my mental health history. I requested a prescription for antidepressant medication as I was really struggling to carry out my duties at work and I was aware how down I was. This led to a telephone appointment and the Dr could not have been more helpful or understanding. She prescribed the medication and I have been taking it since then.

Within a few days the medication started to work, I could feel myself waking from what felt like a form of unpleasant hibernation, or nightmare. The regular use of mental health medication has meant that I have been able to manage my situation in a way that suits me much better. My moods are much more stable, I don't find myself in periods of prolonged low mood and I am more alert.

It has helped me to see scenarios that are likely to trigger me before they happen and either avoid or manage them better. It is one of the most important steps I have taken as far as my own mental health is concerned.

Chapter 7
Let's get down to the nitty gritty!

What is 'mental health'?

So far, this book has been full of waffle about me - the fella you don't know, just another guy on the street. But this book is supposed to be about you. I want to help you learn more about the subject of mental health so that you can help yourself and maybe even other people.

Whether you like it or not, YOU are the most important person in your life and if you fail to look after you properly, you will not be in a position to get the most from life. Nor will you be in a place to successfully help others around you.

It took me too long to work this out.

Mental health is a term used to describe the state of mind we find ourselves in and our ability to undertake tasks and conduct a normal life. It is that simple. It is how you feel 'in yourself' – as we say up north!

What is mental 'ill' health?

Mental ill health is a term used to describe our psychological state when it negatively affects our mood, manner, ability to carry out tasks or operate as we would normally. This usually results in our physical or psychological health being put at risk of harm and it may also put those we meet at risk of harm too.

There are many ways in which we can suffer with mental ill health. We refer to these different ways as 'mental health conditions'. It is not uncommon for more than one condition to occur at once. Common examples of Mental Health conditions include:

- Depression
- Stress
- Anxiety
- Attention Deficit Hyperactivity Disorder (ADHD)
- Dementia
- Grief
- Eating Disorders
- Phobias
- Bipolar Disorder
- Depression
- Schizophrenia
- Post Traumatic Stress Disorder (PTSD)
- Obsessive Compulsive Disorder (OCD)

These are just some of the more well known mental health conditions, but there are many more.

What is mental 'wellbeing'?

Mental 'wellbeing' describes the state of mind we are in, when we can conduct our normal life with a good level of mental functionality without being at risk of harm either physically or psychologically due to the condition of our mental health. This can be demonstrated by how well we can complete tasks successfully, whether we are capable in work and in our career, our ability to enjoy a healthy work life balance, being aware of triggers which may affect our mental health and maintaining a mindful and healthy understanding of our own mental health situation.

How can mental ill health affect us in our day-to-day lives?

The wide variety of mental health conditions comes with an even broader range of symptoms or indicators for those who live with mental illness daily. Symptoms associated with some of the more common mental health conditions include:

- Lack of confidence
- Being short tempered or aggressive
- Loss of appetite or overeating
- Dependency on alcohol, drugs or other stimulants
- Loss of libido
- Loss of concentration
- Withdrawal from society
- Avoiding spending time with family and friends
- Suicidal thoughts

- Violence towards others

I will cover more issues associated with mental health conditions as we go along. The symptoms and issues we encounter can be crippling and they often overlap, making things even worse.

Mental health is like a housing estate

Imagine looking along a street of houses. From the outside, they all look similar, but they never look exactly the same. They may have different coloured windows, front doors, plants in the gardens, etc. This is like us humans. To a stranger, we all look alike on the outside and, besides minor differences, we are all very similar.

Each homeowner has a better knowledge of what's going on within their homes. They know if they have a dripping tap, or a dodgy plug socket. Some people have the skills to fix them, or to pay for someone else to fix them, others live with them, or do not have the skills or resources to have them fixed.

Some people are comfortable asking a friend or someone else down the street to help them get the issues sorted. But there are also people who choose to keep these matters to themselves, which leads to things getting worse, or to other problems which compound the scenario.

There are other types of issue too. The drips and the leaks that cause problems under the floorboards, or behind walls without even the homeowner's knowledge. They might realise that something does not seem right, but they do not know what and they don't know the cause. It may turn out that the house has inbuilt flaws; problems that were not obvious during the build, or that have not affected the property straight away, but they are there.

It is the same with our bodies and minds. The way we treat them, ignore them, or try to fix them can affect their long-term performance. Chemical changes throughout our life can mean that issues come and go. None of us is to blame for that.

Using this analogy to understand and think about human behaviour can be such a useful tool. It can help us to be more forgiving of the behaviours and reactions of others, just as they can be of ours. Society has created a very unhealthy stigma relating to pride and appearance. It forces most of us at one stage or another to wear an outer shell, which does not truly represent our feelings or our situation. This is a physical and literal metaphor, as the clothes we wear or the makeup we put on forms part of this masquerade.

Keeping your windows maintained and well painted and your brass doorknob shiny, tends to make people assume that we are not a person with a leaking tap or a creaky floorboard. I say, so what if we are? If we know about it, but we can still function just fine like that, so what?

Most people have some sort of home maintenance system in place. They will put some money away for repairs and will have their roof tiles replaced when they notice a leak. That management of the home is much like our mind too. By using self-help methods, such as taking part in activities you enjoy, meditating or walking the dog and being more mindful, you are taking positive steps to maintain your mental health, reducing the likelihood of 'a burst pipe', or 'house fire'.

Common misconceptions associated with mental health issues

There is an assumption that people with mental health issues will be miserable, uncooperative, unemployable, aggressive, violent or even suicidal. Victims can become trapped in a cycle of discrimination and isolation, which can be particularly damaging, resulting in their lives spiralling out of control. It is these times that require us to recognise the signs and to make use of some of the practices mentioned in the later chapters of this book. These include healthy routines, eating well, getting enough sleep and being kind to ourselves. All things which I know are easier said than done.

The negative stigma can lead to people being uncomfortable admitting they are suffering with a problem. The knock-on effect of this is that they are unlikely to seek help for the issues that they suffer with, for fear that they become marginalised for the circumstances they find themselves in.

This not only means that they do not get the help they may need and deserve, but it is also likely to mean that others are in the same position and are not speaking up about it.

If a high proportion of people with mental health problems are not seeking help, it is impossible to understand the true scale of the problem. This one of the many reasons mental health services are poorly funded and/or understaffed, leaving them unable to provide support to those who need it.

A whistlestop guide to mental health basics

It is a challenge to write these sections without sounding dry and 'textbooky', but we need to ensure that we are properly informed and capable of handling things appropriately.

What would be helpful is to bring things back to absolute basics as far as mental health is concerned. Helping you to understand, if you don't already, what we mean by mental health; what some of the more common mental health issues are; how they appear; and what we can do to manage them.

Issues associated with our mental health impact on all aspects of our life, affecting our ability to carry out tasks we normally find simple and can have an enormous impact on our relationships with loved ones, friends and colleagues. In addition, the stigma associated with mental health issues could lead us to be shunned, or not given opportunities available to others.

Working to change mental health stereotypes

In recent years, there has been a positive shift in the public's attitude towards the stereotypes associated with mental ill health. Probably because of an improved understanding of mental health issues and better health management. But primarily because several high profile celebrities have spoken out in the media about having and dealing with their own mental health issues.

However, strong links exist between discrimination and the onset of mental health issues relating to factors such as ethnicity, social background and gender. This connection highlights the likelihood of experiencing mental health problems in our lifetime based on our socio-economic background. In many cases, the effects of discrimination and stigma can be as damaging as the mental health problems themselves.

Nearly a third of people under the age of twenty-five who experience mental health problems feel that discrimination is a key factor in them giving up on their ambitions for life. Much of the discrimination they face comes from friends, siblings, parents and people who are part of their lives. I found that some of those close to me really struggled when I was experiencing mental health issues. They struggled to come to terms with this and regularly reminded me that I was not who I used to be. As if I didn't already know that!

Similar patterns exist in older people as well, although these can be harder to identify because of their long-held attitudes shaped by society, the TV they have watched and the jobs they have worked in.

All of this is what I would like to tap into and change through some of the practices and ideas discussed in this book. Nobody should have to struggle because of a perfectly natural circumstance they find themselves in, which has been vilified or seen as a weakness by society and the media over the years.

After my first breakdown, I was not the person I had been previously. Or, perhaps more accurately, I did not seem to be the person I had shown on the outside.

As mentioned, people regularly commented on this and those comments hurt. I really could have done without this when I was recovering, but it is a difficult thing to communicate. I understood that most of the comments came from a good place and that people wanted to see me well, but they did not realise what a punch in the gut it was; to be reminded constantly that you were different now and that they clearly preferred the old guy.

If you experience this, it is important to explain calmly and pleasantly to people that we have been unwell and this may cause us to come across differently; it is not something we are comfortable with and it hurts to be reminded repeatedly about it. But this is easier said than done.

Communication is everything

Probably one of the most basic and yet most difficult methods for supporting you with your mental health conundrums, is to talk to someone you trust. It doesn't have to be your nearest and dearest. It might be a colleague, a friend or even your GP. Being open and talking about things will show you that you are not alone and may reveal that more people than you realise have suffered with their mental health at one time or another.

Chapter 8

Depression

What is depression?

Depression is one of the most common types of mental health condition. A substantial proportion of the UK population will suffer with depression at some point in their lifetime.

It affects different people in different ways and can affect the same person differently at different times in their life. Many of the symptoms of depression also appear in people with other mental health problems and it is common for someone to experience depression and another mental health issue at the same time.

How depression affects me

Depression, "The Black Dog" and mental ill health are very cruel. I imagine them as parasites, feeding on what makes us strong or happy and reducing our ability to be able to get well.

There are chemicals in the brain which regulate our mood. When these chemicals become imbalanced, a person is likely to experience depression. But there is evidence that a combination of medication and lifestyle choices such as diet and exercise, along with brain stimulation, can alleviate many of the symptoms of depression.

There are also genetic influences, meaning that if a person's parents or grandparents suffered with depression, they are more likely to pass this on to their offspring.

In my case, depression causes me to become agoraphobic. I don't want to go out and I don't want to see people, even those I know and like. This includes some of my closest family and friends. I just want to hide away. If I must go out when I am at my worst, I scurry down backstreets and alleyways as quickly as possible (like a rabbit worried a hawk might by flying over) hoping I don't bump into anyone and have to talk to them.

To put this into context, when I am well, I talk to anyone and everyone. Perhaps too much! I'm a big, friendly guy who thrives on social interaction with others. I now know that getting exercise, especially outdoors, has known links with the improvement of mental health. When you're struggling, even with this knowledge, it's challenging to take the brave steps needed to overcome some of the problems you are facing.

Spending time with people you care about and who care about you is another thing which helps with your mental health.

When I am down, I feel like I cannot take part in hobbies I have previously loved and I simply can't concentrate on anything. I can't sit down and watch my favourite movies or TV programs, partly because through anxiety my attention span and my ability to concentrate gets battered.

I also find that I tend to eat excessive amounts and I used to drink more alcohol.

I feel a strong urge to do things I know to be bad, such as spending money on something I can't really afford. I do certain jobs at home, like decorating or furniture building, to provide an excuse for why I can't do the things I know are ultimately more productive.

When I was really unwell, at the horrible job, I would vomit before leaving for work because of anxious energy and worry as I was being bullied and just wanted to stay at home with my family. I also suffered with crippling stomach cramps from irritable bowel syndrome (IBS).

All these things have the knock-on effect of making issues worse in the long term. My fitness levels drop, I gain weight, which makes my injured back more susceptible to failing me and causing me pain. It makes me feel less comfortable being outside and seeing people. At my worst I would walk along muttering to myself, desperately thinking of crazy solutions to get me out of the hole I was in and things just spiraled out of control. Like falling down the inside of one of the spinney charity coin collector things you used to see at the swimming baths. A slow spiral down, inevitably heading for that black hole at the bottom; the lower the coin gets, the faster (or in my case, fatter) it gets until it is out of control and…plop, cha-ching! Into the darkness I went.

Boy, oh boy, was it dark and lonely down there!

Untangling the ball of string

Being stuck in a negative state is exhausting and leaves me feeling desperate. This is usually caused by depression, anxiety, stress or a combination of each. When I feel that way, I really struggle to decide what the next most sensible step forward is. The best way for me to describe this feeling is to ask you to imagine that all the tasks in front of you are like an extremely tangled ball of string. I frantically try to untangle the threads, but all I do is make the situation worse.

The trick is to identify the individual tasks that make up that ball of string. Some are easier to complete and untangle than others, so they are the ones to start with. Once we have done this a few times, we discover that some of the slightly more complicated tasks are easier to confront and complete. Eventually, as confidence increases and the knots loosen, we reach a point where we can manage more than one of these tasks at once and find a way of getting back on track.

This approach has been extremely useful in helping me write this book. There have been moments when it felt overwhelming and I struggled to know what the most appropriate step forward was. Choosing to work on something I know I can do with relative ease has been a way to help keep the project moving.

Once I have completed that task, the next most difficult task seems more achievable and so on. If I am still struggling though, rather than 'wading through treacle', I save what I have done, step away and come back later when I feel more comfortable.

Symptoms of depression

Symptoms of depression include feelings of deep and prolonged unhappiness and hopelessness, resulting in a loss of interest in things that an individual might normally enjoy.

Depression disrupts a person's ability to perform routine tasks. It can interfere with daily life and make tasks that would otherwise be straightforward difficult to accomplish.

It is a common misunderstanding that a person who has depression will appear sad and/or miserable. Interestingly, depression may lead to people overcompensating their outward emotions, seeming larger than life, the life and soul of the party. There may also be no obvious outward signs of the condition at all.

How does this differ from feeling down?

Feeling down or in a low mood is a state of mind which someone is likely to recover from. It is a natural state, but usually short-lived. It is usually a direct response to a scenario to incident that has occurred. Making lifestyle changes, such as sleeping more or dealing with difficult scenarios occurring in life, can improve low mood.

To suffer with depression means to experience recurring feelings of despair and worthlessness. People with depression often choose to remove themselves from what might be considered 'everyday life'. If we are going to address our depression, it is more likely that we would require intervention of some kind, whether that be by medical professionals or other alternative therapies as well as long-term lifestyle changes.

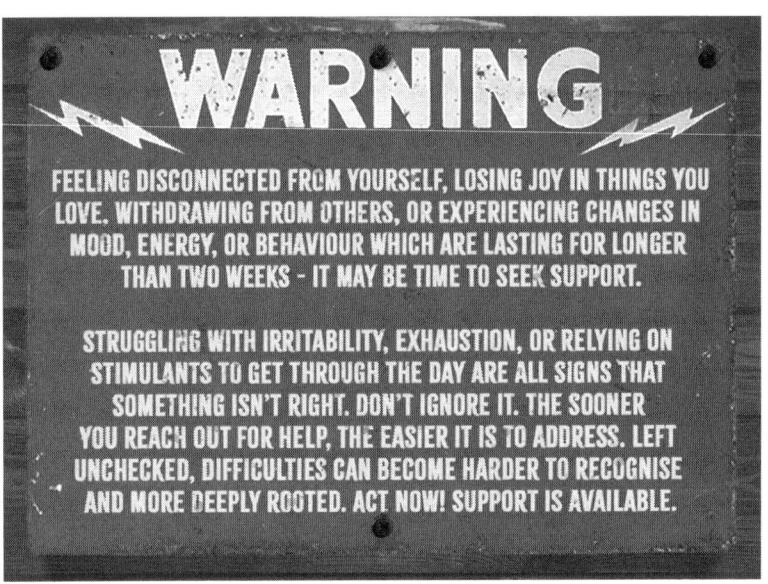

I know that this image has already appeared in chapter two of this book, but it is such an important message and now that we have reached a place that you feel more open about your situation, you might also feel more comfortable acting on the message.

Some causes of depression

There is no definitive single reason which explains why people suffer from depression. The illness can arise for a variety of reasons and different people have different triggers which may negatively impact their mental state.

A combination of life events can trigger depression, such as illness, injury, financial problems, divorce and bereavement, although there are no strict rules for what will and what won't trigger depression.

People have described it to me as being a 'downward spiral' or that they feel trapped and cannot see a way to 'climb out' of their circumstances. I often describe my experience as being caught in a fog, which I simply could not make my way out of. Sometimes the fog got lighter or heavier, but it was always present, preventing me from being able to manage and enjoy my life as I used to.

Other symptoms of depression

I have explained how depression has affected me. Although most people are likely to have a similar experience, they will not all be the same, just as we are all different. Common symptoms of depression include:
- Continuous low mood or sadness
- Feeling hopeless and helpless

- Low self-esteem
- Feeling tearful
- Feeling guilt ridden
- Lack of motivation or interest in things
- Finding it difficult to make decisions
- Not getting any enjoyment out of life
- Feeling anxious or worried
- Suicidal thoughts
- Thoughts of harming yourself

Identify the symptoms you experience from the list above. Using the blank version of the depression diary (available in Chapter 25) keep a note of your own symptoms. You can log the duration and intensity of the symptoms. This will help you to monitor whether or not you might be suffering with depression and if you might need to seek support from someone you trust or a medical professional.

Depression Diary

Symptom	Date	Length of time
Continuous low mood or sadness	15/08/24	All afternoon
	16/08/24	All day
	17/08/24	All day could not sleep
Feeling guilt ridden	15/08/24	All Afternoon
	17/08/24	After dinner
	18/08/24	

How our depression can affect those we care about most

The effects of depression can be wide ranging. We become tired and irritable, are hard to live with and difficult to have a conversation with. We lose the ability to think straight, or in a linear fashion, particularly during our darker periods.

It can be difficult to communicate about these problems when we are struggling with our mental health and it can be equally difficult for our loved ones to be comfortable enough to raise it with us.

It is vitally important for us to share how we feel with those we encounter and love, this includes our family and colleagues. Doing this will help prevent them from worrying that they may be responsible for the changing behaviours.

Depression and the demands of daily life

Depression makes it difficult to handle the various pressures of modern life. Maintaining and affording a home, managing children and holding down a job are all part of everyday life, but they can be stressful. Adding to this, losing a loved one, unemployment, financial difficulties, addiction, illness, or the illness of family or friends; can cause a person with depression to spiral out of control.

Depression is likely to influence all aspects of our life. Sometimes we may not even be aware that we are suffering, or we are aware but try to hide it, often successfully. In my experience, behaving as though there is nothing wrong can make things even more difficult. It feels like I am operating with an 'invisible mask' which can be tiring, lonely and upsetting. This is something I have done throughout my life, often through politeness towards others, but also to disguise my pain and cover what others might perceive to be weakness.

Commonly, depression also affects our diet and appetite, making us eat less or more. This can have a major impact on our health. I have had serious problems with Irritable Bowel Syndrome (IBS), especially in the earlier years. This condition affects many people who struggle with depression and other mental health conditions. It affects the digestive system and can cause stomach cramps, bloating, diarrhoea and constipation.

The effects can last for long periods, but it also comes and goes. IBS can be seriously debilitating. I found the stomach cramps to be excruciating and particularly difficult to deal with in certain scenarios. I once had terrible cramps when driving in the middle of nowhere! They were so bad I had to pull over until they subsided.

There is no known cure for IBS, it is a case of managing it as best we can using medication and changes to our diet. After doing some lifestyle research, I have found that avoiding chili peppers, onions and garlic has made a significant difference to my IBS and I rarely suffer with it as severely as I used to. I make an extra special attempt to avoid these foods during periods when I am struggling with my mental health, to lessen the discomfort the IBS causes.

Depression can often cause us to become tired easily and lose concentration when working on basic tasks. It is common to experience problems in relationships with friends and family. Depression may cause people to turn to drugs or alcohol to try to numb their feelings, however, this ultimately tends to add to their problems.

Sadly, all too often, people suffering with depression resort to suicide even though it could be easily prevented with the correct support.

I don't know precisely when I began to suffer with depression because it crept up on me. I suspect I had always felt some level of depression, so it felt like an extension of what I was used to. This made it so hard for me to recognise. When an emotion or feeling increases in such small increments, there is no obvious 'straw' to break the camel's back. It just gets worse slowly. No alarm goes off when you shift from feeling down to having depression. Your skin doesn't go blue and you don't grow a giant head!

There are resources and treatments available which may help an individual experiencing depression (See the 'Helpful resources' section towards the end of the book for more information and contact details for useful organisations and more)

Suicidal thoughts

I thought long and hard about including this section in my book. The last thing I want to do is put ideas in anyone's head. But equally, it is too important to leave out.

Recently I spoke with a friend on this subject. A friend who, like me, has struggled with mental health issues but was not comfortable sharing them with people. We both agreed that, even at our lowest point, we had never been in a place where we felt we were actively planning to take our own lives. I want to share this, as it would be wrong of me not to be thoroughly honest to you, the reader.

But we also admitted that we had both encountered suicidal thoughts. We had considered whether the world and our loved ones would be in a better place if we were no longer here. Both of us had considered methods of taking our own lives.

Incredibly, when you discuss this subject with people, you discover that most people know someone who has taken their own life. Often someone they cared deeply about. Suicide leaves a vast hole in people's lives. A loss of this kind is heartbreaking.

I have seen first-hand the impact that a decision like this has upon loved ones. This knowledge and experience helped me to understand how much the people around me loved me and relied upon me spiritually, practically and financially. This realisation kept me from allowing these thoughts to get the better of me.

As I have said before, I am not a specialist in this area, but what I do know for sure is that whoever you are, however bad you feel and no matter how much you hurt; there is a future for you. It may be a journey to get to where you need to be, but you will get there. And there will be people there who are everything to you.

You are loved.
You are wanted.
You are needed.

Today will soon be yesterday.

By working together we can make the mental health discussion as comfortable and commonplace as talking about our physical health. There should be no taboos or judgement and we should be able to take the mickey out of each other and help each other through. If we are going to be able to get there, I am going to need the help of every single person who reads my book.

There are countless charities and support mechanisms out there for people who are feeling this way and I promise that there will be help available to you through mental health services such as the Samaritans and Crisis (See the 'Helpful resources' section towards the end of the book for more information and contact details for these organisations and more).

The Pie Eating Man's approach to depression

There is a fine line between stubbornly avoiding seeking or accepting help and desiring not to be categorised or defined by our mental illness.

One reason I have been able to manage my mental health effectively at work and with friends and colleagues is that I was determined not to be held back by what was essentially a brain illness or injury.

Around the time that I handed in my notice at the horrible job (see Chapter 5), I could not see how I was going to get myself out of the hole I was in. I certainly could not see how I might flourish in life, but I did - one step at a time.

That's the best way to overcome these large obstacles. In the many tales of extraordinary survival that have taken place throughout history, those who survived against all odds almost always say that you must set yourself small achievable targets and never give up. A phrase I like to use is that you can't eat a whole pizza in one bite, but nibble by nibble it is not an overwhelming task.

Don't look at the bigger picture, break it down into smaller more manageable parts. Then you can just take each small win at a time. They will add up. It worked for me and it can work for you!

Just take the "effing" tablets man!

Remember in Chapter 6, when I talked about my recovery from my first breakdown? I mentioned I rebelled against taking the tablets prescribed by the G.P. Twenty-five years later, I still regret this. Not taking the tablets was a bad idea and I am sure I lost out because of my decision. It wasn't until my second breakdown in 2020 that I started taking mental health medication.

I had been advising people who came to me for support that they should go to their GP and consider taking medication, yet I wasn't doing that myself. What a hypocrite!

When I finally started taking them, what a difference those tablets made to me. They evened out the peaks and troughs of emotions; helped to remove the fog and the confusion and my inner monologue became so much more kind towards me and others. They allowed me to forgive and understand more easily and helped me to stick up for myself and make better decisions. Medication may not be for everyone, but I heartily recommend you consider this option with an open mind.

Chapter 9

Stress

What is stress?

Stress is the state the body finds itself in when responding to difficult circumstances; caused by physical or mental pressures, or in some cases a combination of the two. Stress can be short-lived or can continue for extended periods.

Emotional hijack by our own brain!!!

There is a part of our brain which is called the Amygdala. It is where our brains 'fear management' centre is located.

One thing the amygdala does is to manage our natural panic stations by deciding whether our brain needs to pump adrenaline into our body so that we can stand and fight or run like hell. This is known as our 'fight-or-flight' response.

When this happens our brain ignores the prefrontal cortex, which is where the logical decisions are made. Meaning that our ability to make sensible decisions about whether the bank statement in front of us really has the ability to kill us, is lost. Which is why they make us feel so awful.

I want people to know that stress does not belong to them. What I mean by that is that there should be no guilt associated with stress, or any other mental health conditions for that matter. By attributing guilt to a condition like stress, we basically sprinkle some more stress on top of the stress that already exists. Feeling guilty about stress is to all intents and purposes like feeling guilty about blinking when the wind blows sand towards us. They are both natural reactions to a scenario that we have been exposed to.

By understanding that stress is something we are programmed to do for good reason; it is something that we can then limit the impact of, by removing the burden of shame.

What causes stress?

Many situations can lead to what we commonly refer to as 'stress'. What these situations usually have in common is that they typically arise because of an excess of some external factor. For example.

- Working long hours and not taking sufficient rest for to allow your body and/or mind to recover sufficiently.
- Becoming a parent and trying to meet the demands of a new baby on top of all the normal demands of life. This might include more children and a partner. In this scenario, everybody will probably experience stress, which is likely to make things even worse than if it was just you.

- Uncertainty: not knowing what may happen in the future regarding relationships, health, careers, or even your chosen football team's results! All these things can put people in a state of uncertainty, which will ultimately cause them stress.
- A combination of the pressures of normal life, trying to maintain a reasonable work life balance while dealing with deadlines, difficult colleagues, expensive bills, debts, etc.

I am sure that you can add to this list.

Harmful impacts of stress

It's a widely known fact that increased exposure to stress can have a negative impact on an individual's overall health. Stress usually stimulates the body by increasing the heart rate, which increases blood-flow around the body. This provides more oxygen to the brain and/or muscles and improves their ability to react if needed.

Stress can release a surge of hormones, including adrenaline, epinephrine and cortisol. Although these hormones can provide the body with useful stimulation for short periods, long-term exposure can have a negative effect on blood pressure, the heart and arteries. The release of these hormones and the combined effect of stress cause tiredness after their effects have dissipated and over long periods of stress, they can cause exhaustion and fatigue.

Unhealthy levels of stress can cause the brain to release a hormone called cortisol, ongoing exposure to cortisol causes us to crave salty, sugary and high fat 'comfort' foods. Cortisol can also produce a resistance to insulin in the body, which can cause the body to store abdominal or 'visceral' fat.

Storage of fat in the belly area is considered to pose increased risk of serious medical issues.

The long-term effects of stress and visceral fat on the body can increase the chance of experiencing depression, anxiety, heart disease, Alzheimer's, cancer, type two diabetes, stroke and high cholesterol.

Positive effects of stress

We usually consider stress to be a negative condition that we suffer from, however its original purpose is supposed to be useful to us as humans. Stress is a part of the fight-or-flight mechanism built into the human brain. Its purpose is to provide the body and the brain with the chemicals needed in a high-pressure situation, to allow us to be alert and perform at our best according to the scenario. We may need to overcome a problem mentally or require additional energy to escape a situation physically.

Stress can make an individual more alert so they can notice danger or discover a food source. It can boost our memory, allowing the recollection of previous events, or improving our ability to store memories for the future. Stress can allow the body to improve the function of certain body parts and organs to help fight illness and infection.

Symptoms of stress

Common symptoms of stress include butterflies, anxiety, insomnia, sweating, aches and pains, heart palpitations and high blood pressure. Often, people confuse these symptoms with other illnesses because stress can be a byproduct of a different condition they are suffering from, such as an infection or depression.

Stress can lower the body's immune system, leaving an individual more likely to be susceptible to other illnesses.

How does stress affect us?

As far as mental health is concerned, there is often an overlap between the conditions themselves and the issues they cause.

Often, an individual will suffer with stress and anxiety; it is hard to separate the two. They share many symptoms, including IBS, diarrhoea, headaches, allergies, heart disease, shortness of breath, panic attacks, high blood pressure and stomach ulcers.

Someone who suffers with stress may find that it affects all aspects of their life; their ability to sleep and concentrate, putting a strain on relationships and their profession.

Stress from external factors which might be considered more physical in nature can also cause us psychological stress. If we are already experiencing stress from our work, or the people around us, the addition of external sources of stress can make things even worse.

Physical or external factors which result in, or exacerbate, stress on an individual include:

- Exposure to extreme temperatures.
- Being kept awake for long periods of time.
- Injuries and illness particularly those which are serious or affect a person long term.
- Physical exhaustion caused by excess activity.
- A lack of food or water.
- Second Hand Stress or Transference of Stress.

> ### Stress Scenarios
>
> I have experienced stress over long periods. For example working at the horrible job, I was exposed to bullying daily. I felt exhausted all of the time and ultimately this caused me to experience my first breakdown.
>
> Another example I can think of was after a serious car accident on a 60mph country road. The boost of cortisol and adrenaline I experienced straight after that led me to try and chase after the car which had caused the accident and left the scene! That car was travelling at 60 mph too, so I had no chance of catching it. It was the effects of the accident that I believe had left me slightly delirious.
>
> When I realised that it was not possible to catch the car, I began desperately asking passing drivers to chase and catch them. Only when the adrenaline started to wear off did I realise that parts of my body were in pain. Approximately 1 hr later I was exhausted.

Second hand stress

Like a contagious disease, stress can be infectious. We can catch it from other people we spend time with who are displaying signs of it. This is because we have a natural tendency to want to empathise and help people who are in distress. We reflect their behaviours in our own.

To help understand this, picture one of those TV shows where people capture others on camera, doing crazy and dangerous things either on purpose or by accident. When you see someone fall off a skateboard and smash their nuts on a park bench or observe somebody go flying off a snow mobile into a tree, there is a split second when you almost feel the pain that they feel. Our brains behave similarly when we are with people showing signs of stress. The brain releases the same stress related chemicals even if we are not directly involved in the situation.

There are ways to manage second hand stress. A great start is to be more present and observant in difficult situations. The ability to consciously identify the signs that are occurring which we pick up on and mirror, rather than unconsciously is very important. It is a form of being triggered, although it is less personal to us as observers which can make it harder to identify.

Other ways to manage stress also work for second hand stress.

It helps to be comfortable with who we are, having a job or tasks that we can manage, having a good work/life balance and having things to look forward to. We are more susceptible to second hand stress when we are unsettled and stressed ourselves.

In situations that cause us to feel like we might be inheriting stress from someone; it is worth doing what we can to remove ourselves from the problem. By taking 'a breather' or a short walk down the street to the shop, you can let the dust settle before you return. Find a piece of work to concentrate on or put your headphones in and listen to some music that calms you down or distracts you. You could plan to work in the office on a different day than that person.

You might want to consider helping the individual get out of the situation they find themselves in, so that neither of you feels stressed anymore. This strategy comes with Huge WARNING though. These scenarios can be like quicksand and just like in the TV programs from my childhood, it can be easier to be pulled into the situation than it is to pull the person out.

If you find it difficult to shake off some of these emotions, or if you feel you are picking up on other people's stress more and more, it might be worth going to see a doctor to discuss this. The chances are that it is hitting you more than you realise and it might be something that you can follow basic steps to improve.

Support could be available through medication or alternative therapies, such as talking therapy, hypnotherapy, even a change of diet.

Self-care measures are always useful and can help, particularly if there is a wait between referrals and appointments made by your GP. Take time out to relax, go for a walk in a green space, try and get childcare so that you can meditate in peace; or listen to Megadeath at full blast! Whatever works for you.

There are so many alternatives available, but the hardest part is recognising the symptoms and granting yourself permission to seek a solution.

Most of the coping mechanisms discussed in Chapters 10, 11 and 12 will be useful to you when trying to manage second hand stress.

Interestingly, increased stress levels can trigger this condition, which can further elevate anxiety levels, creating a harmful combination. Evidence also shows that depression can heighten activity in the amygdala, a phenomenon known as emotional or amygdala hijack.

Chapter 10

Anxiety

What is anxiety?

Anxiety is a feeling of unease that often comes with worry or fear. Sometimes there is an obvious reason for it and sometimes there isn't. Anxiety can range from mild and brief to severe and long-lasting.

What is a panic attack?

A panic attack is when a person experiences feelings of overwhelming anxiety, terror, or fear, forcing them to try to avoid the scenario they are in at all costs. Panic attacks usually come with physical symptoms, which can include hyperventilation; hot and cold flushes; numbness and/or tingling, particularly in the arms, hands and feet; dizziness, nausea and sweating, amongst other things.

What causes anxiety?

Almost anything can bring on feelings of anxiety. The likelihood of experiencing feelings of anxiety can be increased because of genetics. Some people are simply more susceptible to anxiety than others.

Drugs and stimulants are a common cause of anxiety, both legal, such as caffeine, cigarettes and alcohol, or illegal, such as cocaine, marijuana and heroin. These drugs create an artificial high and the 'come down' from them can cause anxiety, leading to a need to use more. If you become addicted to these kinds of drugs, a lack of them in your system can also cause serious anxiety as well as other physical issues.

External issues caused by work and family or other obligations can also cause anxiety.

You may know the cause of your own anxiety, such as an upcoming event or task and once you address it, you may start feeling better again. However, maybe you have too many tasks on the go at once and this causes anxiety for you. When this is the case, it can be harder to identify the cause. As I have already mentioned with other mental health issues, they can combine and overlap, causing greater difficulty when trying to identify a cause.

Worry

Worry is to anxiety what low mood is to depression. It forms one of the emotional building blocks of anxiety, but it is a temporary condition.

I believe that 'worry' has to be the most frustrating emotion of all. Strangely I don't always associate worry with anxiety, when really they are very similar. Perhaps in my mind, I separate the two with the thought that anxiety is a mental health condition and worry is more a thought process.

For other people I see that worry is a very real thing and I think that my take on it may be flawed. However, by separating them I feel like I have more control over whether or not I worry. So maybe this is a way of managing worry that others could also adopt?

My general approach to worry, or the merest sniff of it, is to act upon the thing that is threatening to cause me to worry. Solve the problem or at least start working towards solving the problem that is creating that worry. This is most likely because I operate with a positive attitude towards life and how I manage it. Worry saps my energy, it distracts me and lowers the chance of me performing at my best, creating distraction and tiredness.

Using my anxiety to do good

I have had a beard since I was twenty one, this is because I had major surgery on my top and bottom jaws. It left me feeling uncomfortable with my appearance when I looked in a mirror. Not feeling I looked like me anymore really affected my mental health.

To manage the anxiety I had relating to my face, I found a solution that suited me. I grew a beard! Since that time my beard has become an important part of my identity. Especially over the last ten years when I have grown it long (Sorry/not sorry mum). People seem to know me as the beard guy.

I have only shaved my beard off a couple of times since I was twenty one, once in 2016 when I raised around £800.00 for Cancer Research. Once a week before lockdown as I was always touching my face, I went and got the illness a week later ☹.

In 2022 I offered Nikki, the founder of My Black Dog, to grow it for a year and shave it off at CarFest to raise money and awareness for the charity.

People often think that having a big beard shows I have confidence, but for me not having a beard is like walking down the street naked. My beard gives me confidence, it has become my shield and security blanket. As mentioned it is now a part of my identity. To shave it off was a really big thing for me. However if you think of the difficult issues many people have to face on a daily basis, to shave my beard off is a mere token by comparison. In the end and with the help of Chris Evans and the Virgin Breakfast Show team, I raised nearly £3000.00 for My Black Dog (See photos 11 and 12 in the Photos section).

Manifestation

You may have heard of people using the word 'Manifestation'. This is another phrase which has the potential of being thought of as a bit 'woo woo' but in my opinion there is reason behind Manifestation and it links with worry. Let me explain.

The act of manifestation is when we focus our thoughts and aims on a specific goal or outcome. Some people think that by doing this, that goal or outcome will magically appear, which is obviously not the case. However, by focusing our mindset in order to identify and seize opportunities that will help us to achieve those goals, it is more likely to make them attainable.

This book is a perfect example of this. I started thinking about writing this book in the summer of 2022, however, it was not until Early in 2024 that I actually took the time to seriously put pen to paper, (or fingers to keyboard to be more accurate) and started to write it. Now in August 2024 it is pretty much finished. This is because it has remained in my 'sights' and has been my primary aim, outside of work for the past five months or so. I have used the advantages that have been made available to me and the time I have had to spare, to tap away and get it done. I could have spent the past five months or so thinking, "Urgh, I just don't have it in me to write a book, so I'll just have another Hobnob and watch the telly". So many people have said to me, "I'd love to write a book, but I'll never do it", I now know that, if they think that way, that is what they will manifest.

I think worry works in a similar way, by dwelling on the negative, or the things that could go wrong and not using that as a tool to overcome the obstacles in front of us. I think that worry becomes a negative manifestation.

There are many things in our lives that we cannot control and to worry about those is a waste of time and energy, as they either will or will not happen whether we worry about them or not. However, managing things that are within our control rather than worrying about them is far more likely to be of benefit to us.

Be careful when using social media

Avoid using your phone and social media when you are working. Consider allowing yourself set times for use of your devices and try to draw clear lines of separation in between those times. When eating, when walking the dog (he says as he types this into his phone on a dog walk, desperately hoping his precariously balanced phone doesn't shoot into the air and land in some dog-dooky).

When you spend time on social media, make sure you align yourself with positive and interesting groups. The more positive stuff you do, the more positive the algorithms will get. There are lots and lots of groups where you can connect with people who share your interests. Be careful though, as even some of those can be toxic.

Exam Anxiety

I do not enjoy exams. Despite having excellent memory of incidents and scenarios from my past, right back to when I was younger than 18 months old, I just can't seem to recall information in the way you need to in order to pass exams. In my opinion, exams are a poor and unfair measurement of somebody's knowledge or capability.

So, when I am required to prepare for and undertake exams, I become overwhelmed by anxiety. Often I am not even aware that I am anxious until I notice various behaviours which I recognise as signs.

These include 'ticks', involuntary movements of parts of my body, particularly my hands and wrists. I chew the inside of my lips until they become sore.

Strangely I do these things when I am excited too. Which shows how closely linked these emotions are, and how different emotions are managed by similar parts of the brain, producing the same bodily reactions.

When I suffer with anxiety, aside from the physical effects mentioned, I get butterflies in my stomach. I become more irritable than normal and I have less patience. I don't sleep well, and I can wake in the night in a cold sweat, fixated on the issue which is causing my anxiety.

Ways to manage anxiety

The most important thing we can do to help ourselves manage our anxiety is to recognise that it is affecting us.

Then we need to acknowledge that we want to change our circumstances.

Once we have done this, we need to decide if there is anything holding us back from trying to recover. If so, we must try to deal with that.

A good place to start is by establishing why we would like to improve our circumstances. Examples might include career goals, being a good example to our family or wanting to have the confidence to see our friends more.

'Climbing out' of anxiety might include the need to set short and long-term targets, making sure not to be too ambitious too quickly. Recovery is all about manageable baby steps.

Another helpful step towards reducing the effects of anxiety is sharing our concerns with someone we trust. It may help to share the feelings we are having and the problems we face regarding anxiety. People often say 'a problem shared is a problem halved' and that's true, as long as the person you're sharing with is someone you can trust.

Asking for help should never be seen as a weakness.

Give yourself space

Finding space to relax and enjoy mindful activities, such as hobbies we love or physical exercise, is an excellent way to reduce anxiety and maintain recovery. Modern life often exposes people to high levels of stress and low levels of physical activity, but if we can tip the balance the opposite way we will find it easier to manage stress and anxiety.

How finding positives can help to reduce anxiety

Anxiety generally arises from fear or worry and the more we focus on it, the more we will get pulled into the vortex of negative thinking. Negative thought patterns create more negative thought patterns. They increase the levels of anxiety and make it harder to solve problems rationally. Overwhelming levels of anxiety leave us debilitated and unable to continue with basic problem solving.

Maintaining a positive demeanour not only helps us to see and take advantage of opportunities we think we may benefit from; it also helps to make people around us feel we can be trusted and relied upon to do things. This continues the positive cycle and encourages more external investment from others.

Maintaining a positive demeanour and 'wearing a mask' are close bedfellows and the latter can be dangerous if we don't have someone to confide in. It can be easy to find comfort in hiding our true feelings, when we should be sharing them.

Anxiety management activities

It is important to know that anxiety may make undertaking enjoyable activities harder at first. However, with practice and by making regular slots to take time out, it should be possible for us to get more out of these activities. Outdoor exercise is an activity that can improve mental health and reduce stress and anxiety. Whether you do it alone, with a friend, loved one or in a group.

Actively taking a break from busy activities, such as work and driving, to relax and be mindful is a popular way for us to reduce anxiety. These activities don't have to be complex or expensive. Many people find comfort in simple tasks like walking their dog, or gardening.

Time out

Taking part in meditation, or listening to music, or even just sitting in a quiet space, inside, or outside can help to clear our mind. Deep breathing exercises can be an excellent way of relieving anxiety (more on this later in the book).

Talking therapy

There are two common types of talking therapy they are Cognitive Behavioural Therapy (CBT) and Applied Relaxation Therapy (ART).

CBT is where we discuss our thoughts and attitudes and how they influence how we feel. By drawing links between scenarios and feelings we can find ways of developing coping mechanisms for dealing with different issues that may arise. It's a means of gathering evidence about our feelings and the potential explanations behind them.

ART is a method for teaching us relaxation for specific muscles and muscle groups within the body. We can apply this during periods when we might normally experience anxiety.

This brings me to the final point and possibly the most important as far as mental health goes - DO NOT WORRY ABOUT WHAT OTHER PEOPLE THINK, OR DO. Comparing yourself with others is an entirely fruitless task.

Actor Sir Anthony Hopkins once said:

"My philosophy is, it's none of my business what people say of me and think of me. I am what I am and I do what I do. I expect nothing and accept everything. And it makes life so much easier."

I know that this can seem much easier said than done. However, it is possible to teach yourself to think this way by default. As with most things it takes practice. It is important not to lose empathy for others in the process. Learning to be more aware of the moment and how you can make the best of it is a wonderfully freeing feeling and should help with feelings of anxiety.

Chapter 11

Negativity

We can't really talk about Depression, Stress and Anxiety without inviting along the subject of Negativity for a chat too. It is the shadow which lies beneath all of these mental health struggles, as well as many others. It is stubborn, it is hard to ignore, but you can beat it.

Life is tough

It's no secret that over the past two decades life has got much harder for most people. Each day every one of us is affected by the increasing pressures created by the difficulties of the outside world. These pressures have driven division on a national scale, pushing apart friends, families and colleagues. Things have to change if they are going to improve. I aim to overcome these difficulties by listening and communicating without judgement or blame. I have spent too long being angry in my life and our time here is finite; so for me to waste any more time on such negative emotions is something I am keen to avoid.

Negative thoughts

I expect that we all have that little voice inside our head which questions our decisions and even talks us out of doing things, making us worry or fear the possible negative outcomes, no matter how small they might be.

A carry-over from our evolutionary development, we tend to focus on our worries and concentrate on what could go wrong. Remember in evolutionary terms, it really isn't that long since we lived in caves. Living those primitive lives, we had to find food in periods of famine, fight off giant sloths and ensure we were warm enough. Failing to be prepared for these things meant the difference between life and death for us and those around us.

Back in those days, blindly chasing a mammoth off a cliff or breaking a limb while wrestling an opposing tribe member, could be life threatening.

These were serious concerns for our Neanderthal mind. This is the source of the worry we take to bed with us in modern times or wake up with in the middle of the night. The system was designed to keep us on our toes.

These thoughts not only undermine our ability to make decisions on important matters, but they can also be toxic to our health. They raise our blood pressure and make it more difficult to 'see off' illness.

Managing negative thoughts is difficult and it's a bit like a derelict piece of land; the longer you ignore it, the more overgrown it becomes. Those negative thoughts grow and become like unmanageable bramble bushes, that even when you cut them back, if you don't continue to keep on top of them, they will return twice as thick and with even more voracious thorns.

What is negative bias?

As we have already mentioned, adults naturally tend to focus on negative information as a priority over positive information. This is a natural psychological phenomenon which psychologists refer to as 'negative bias'.

Basically, our amygdala is up to its old tricks again!

Nowadays, health and safety regulations protect us from most of the mortal dangers we encounter (apart from doner kebabs). Our food is available from hygienically packaged containers from the supermarket chilled section. The mortgage we worry about cannot physically hurt us yet these have become our metaphorical sabre-toothed tigers, leaving us with restrictive thoughts bouncing around our heads.

Our response to negative bias can contribute to the problem, making it 'contagious.' People around us are likely to mirror our behaviour and adopt a similar attitude. Can you believe that, negativity is actually 'contagious'?.

Managing negative bias

To manage negative bias, there are two things we need to know.

First, we can take comfort in knowing it is a perfectly normal and natural response.

Second, once we know that humans have a built in, unconscious tendency to focus on the negatives, we can make a conscious effort to recognise that this is what is happening and work to override the instinct. This is a very similar process to managing our triggers, which is something we are going to learn more about in chapter 12.

Our inner voice is a $h17h34d!

I have mentioned that we all have that voice inside our head questioning decisions and talking us out of doing things, creating uncertainty in our minds. Some refer to the inner voice as their 'inner critic', I prefer to call mine, 'that $h17h34d'.

That $h17h34d tries to undermine us, he is the person that persuades us not to apply for that job which is ten miles away and which we would be perfectly good at, because someone better is likely to apply for it. Or because we would miss the two hundred mile drive to work that we currently do every day.

Managing the $h17h34d

One way to quiet the inner voice is to try to cut it out altogether. If you find that you are wrangling with your inner voice and struggling to make a decision, take a piece of paper and write a list of reasons why it is a good idea and do the same for why it might not be. If the list of reasons for outweighs that of against, then you should consider it.

The list is a hard copy of your thoughts, both for and against. That $h17h34d only exists in your head. By physically recording the decision making process in real life, you reduce the influence that $h17h34d can have on undermining your thoughts.

As always, it's a good idea run your ideas past a trusted friend or family member for a second opinion.

I have used this method a number of times in work, or when embarking on big decisions like buying a new home. I have done it a lot of times during the writing of this book, because I care about it and I want it to be right for you. The $h17h34d generally only appears when you are making decisions or plans about things you really care about, oh and when you are walking past the pie shop and you know that you really shouldn't. The solution to that one is though, don't walk past the pie shop unless you are prepared to risk it.

Imposter syndrome

That $h17h34d also plays a part in a very common condition that many struggle with, a condition called Imposter Syndrome. Imposter Syndrome is the feeling you get, generally in work or a position of responsibility. It causes us to doubt our abilities in carrying out our role even when we know we have all the relevant qualifications and those around us have complete confidence in us. Imposter Syndrome does not have to relate to a position which is new, it can be something we live with every day, or it can manifest after we have been in our role for many years.

It is basically that $h17h34d again, making us question whether we can do what is expected of us and the fear of the possible outcomes if we fail.

Most people have areas of work that they feel they are less confident about. It is these areas that the $h17h34d likes to wriggle into and plant the seeds of doubt. Depending on the severity of the self-doubt, we may be able to use similar management techniques to those mentioned in the section above about our inner voice. However, serious cases may require more professional intervention through counselling or even medical assistance.

I suffer with Imposter Syndrome, so do lots of people I speak with. As with many mental health conditions communication with people you trust can often be the key to unlocking this issue. Just don't ask the $h17h34d.

Vortex of negative thinking

When people experience mental health issues such as anxiety, stress and depression, they often struggle with negative thoughts. My own experiences have shown that suffering with depression and anxiety can become overwhelming and form a vortex of negative thinking, which quickly spins out of control.

In normal circumstances, when a person is in good mental health they can see a balance of positive and negative factors which influence their lives. When we are suffering with anxiety, we have a propensity to think more negatively and behave in a more negative fashion. Behaving in such a way can mean that we do not seek to better ourselves because of self-doubt, or we don't think we are good enough to take on a new task. These feelings often result in a psychological downward spiral, lowering our self-esteem a little more each time. It often requires intervention from outside to help someone escape this downward spiral.

It was heartbreaking for me in the horrible job, working in a toxic environment. I would apply for other jobs; jobs I knew I would be good at and, if I was the best version of myself I would easily walk into. The vortex of negative thinking left me in a place where I was a tired and battered version of myself, unable to present the version of me that the employers needed to see. Every time this happened and I didn't get the job I went for, I became even more downhearted.

The curse of negativity

Negativity is a real bugbear of mine. It's one of my biggest triggers in daily life. I am not good at tolerating it. This is my bad! There is method in my madness, though.

I fear that being regularly exposed to negative behaviour could cause me to slip back into a dark place and that is something I must protect myself against.

Remaining positive

Responding to negativity with more negativity is a foolproof way of making the world a worse place and it will make you feel bad. If this pattern continues, it will soon become habitual and before you know it, it will be your automatic response, even to positive situations. If there is one thing that I am certain of, it is that negativity will never cure negativity, nor will it help with positivity.

However, we can overcome negativity with understanding, kindness and a positive approach. The best and easiest example of this is road rage. Something that we all experience at some point. If it happens - say sorry! Don't get cross. If the other person remains cross, this is out of your hands. If you get cross, you might carry this with you for the rest of the day and it is totally needless. Furthermore, the encounter can then affect how safely you are driving for the rest of your journey.

Chapter 12
Trauma and triggers

Trauma before triggers

Trauma is the way that our mind and body respond to an event or incident which cause us great stress or to be in fear for our safety.

Before I start to talk about triggers it is probably sensible to talk a little bit about trauma. Triggers tend to come about as a result of trauma that occurs during an earlier time in our life.

Let me give you a couple of examples of trauma that have affected me, to help you to understand.

Trauma

When I was around fourteen, my mum bought me my first mountain bike, it was a beautiful bike. It was second hand and it was the best bike I had ever ridden, never mind owned. To say that I was chuffed with it was an understatement, I adored it.

It had Shimano gears and was blue colour at the front and went through a kind of rainbow transition to be luminous yellow at the back. One evening, after I had owned the bike for around two weeks, my friend and I went for a bike ride. We rode to a nearby park on the edge of a pretty rough estate. We were looking at some ducklings when we heard a voice shout. "Oi, leave them alone!" We looked up and a group of around six to eight older lads approached us. Obviously we were only looking at the ducklings because they were cute, we were not harming them in any way. These lads were just looking for a fight. I was no shrinking violet and would normally have stuck up for myself, but there were too many of them, most of them looked older than us, they looked hard and were clearly from the nearby estate.

Unfortunately through pure bad luck, we had both stopped with our front wheels right at the bottom of a steep incline. Because of the hill we couldn't just set off and speed away. I remember trying to push down the peddles so hard without making it obvious but the incline was just too steep. The lads came over and told us to leave the ducks alone and one showed a knife, two others punched both me and my friend in the head a few times.

At this point they backed off and we started to ride home.

We had to ride along a long straight bypass home. The bypass had allotments on one side and playing fields on the other, so there were no people around.

We had cycled hard and were nearly back when I looked over my shoulder and two people were coming up behind us on one bike. I looked at my friend and said, "Phew, I thought it was those lads for a second". We both looked again and to our dismay it was, they had caught up with us. They jumped off their bike and one pulled out a knife demanding that I get off my bike. I did. He got on it and they both rode away.

I was gutted. I was frightened and when I say I was gutted, I was really, really gutted.

From that day until I was around thirty, I was unable to

sleep with my windows open at night. Even now I find it very unsettling when people approach me on a footpath from behind on a bike. These are the triggers which were caused by the trauma of the above scenario.

Triggers

You will notice that when talking about mental health, mood and social interaction, it is common to hear people talk about 'triggers' or being 'triggered'. For anyone who does not talk about these subjects very often, these phrases may seem alien.

A trigger is called a trigger because it tends to be a bit like a switch, something which happens and has knock-on effects on an individual straight away.

Triggers tend to be something which negatively impact a person's mental health. In some instances these can be hard to notice, maybe like a 'dripping tap' of lots of small triggers, keeping a person in prolonged low mood.

However, they are more commonly associated with causing the rapid flare up of a person's mental health issues. They create stress and anxiety, which can lead to very serious uncontrollable outbursts, reactions and mood swings.

It can be a specific scenario, or the behaviour of others that causes someone to feel triggered.

Being aware of the things that trigger us is enormously valuable. Triggers influence us to react in a certain way. Once we know what our triggers are, we can work towards managing them and how we react to them. This is a huge step forward in the management of our mental health.

> ### Trigger caused by previous trauma
>
> When I had the horrible job and my boss was making things difficult for me, something they used to do regularly was to ask what I had planned to do for the day?
>
> I always had lots to do, but found it hard to recall the list of things I had to do because of the state I was in. I knew it would mean more work on top of the workload I was already struggling with.
>
> Now when someone asks me this question, it acts as a 'trigger' for me. It takes me back to that same feeling. It can make me withdraw, or even become agitated because of the history I associate with this request.

Have a think about 'what' or maybe 'who' your triggers are and make a note of them on the blank sheet provided in Chapter 25. Each time you come across one make a note of it as they can crop up in the strangest of places. As I have said, once you know what they are you can try to manage them, or eradicate them altogether.

Often the way to eradicate these triggers is through communication this can involve asking people not to do things which cause you to be triggered. I have asked my wife and colleagues not to ask me the "What jobs have you got on today?" question. If they want help with something, I'd much rather that they ask for help with it, as nine times out of ten I will just help no matter what I have planned for the day.

The most effective way I have found to manage many of my triggers, even better than avoiding triggering scenarios, is actually taking a look at those triggers and seeing if I can eradicate them all together.

I do this by asking, "Am I being unreasonable or over sensitive?" In many instances you will probably find that the answer to this question is yes. If that is the case, I consider whether I need to be more tolerant and change my ways, or become more accepting of the trigger.

Am I triggered because the behaviour comes from some historic trauma? Or am I being triggered because I have had a bad day?

Our triggers can even be inherited from those around us. We might do tasks in a certain way, because that's how our parents or teachers showed us to do them. It doesn't necessarily mean that a different way is wrong just that it was not the way we were taught. So we also need to ask ourselves, is someone or something going to come to harm, because of the way something is being done and that is the basis for my trigger? Or, am I simply echoing something that my mum used to be annoyed by and really it's not an issue?

Chapter 13

Attention Deficit Hyperactivity Disorder (ADHD)

What is ADHD?

ADHD or attention deficit hyperactivity disorder is a behavioural condition. Those of us with the condition often act in a way that makes us seem restless. We generally don't like to sit around and do the same thing for long periods and we can struggle to concentrate. We can act impulsively and often seek to get on with things, rather than sit around and discuss them.

Who is likely to be diagnosed with ADHD?

There are specific categories of people who seem to be more susceptible to ADHD than others.

There is an increased chance of being diagnosed with ADHD if a relative has been diagnosed with the condition. If an expectant mother uses drugs, alcohol and/or nicotine during their pregnancy the chances of the baby being diagnosed with ADHD are increased. Babies who are born prematurely are more likely to be diagnosed with ADHD and the likelihood of being diagnosed with ADHD is at least four times greater in males than in females.

In my opinion an ADHD diagnosis can be the beginning of great things! As with everything we do, if we have a better understanding, we can find the most effective way of managing our situation. I think we should all strive to see these diagnoses as something we make the best of, as opposed to seeing them as something which might hold us back.

What are the causes of ADHD?

There are several scenarios that are believed to cause and/or affect whether a person is likely to have ADHD. It is true to say however that the cause of ADHD is not fully understood.

It is thought that Genetics play a part in the likelihood of a person being diagnosed with ADHD and it is common to find that someone with ADHD will also have a close relative or relatives who also have the condition.

Diet and in particular certain colours and preservatives, along with sugars are believed to affect some people with the condition. The Food Standards Agency (FSA) have shown that certain artificial colours and preservatives can increase the likelihood of Hyperactivity in people, particularly children. This has led to laws relating the control of certain additives and 'E' numbers in foods as they are believed to exacerbate the symptoms. This was the case for me growing up and my diet, or indeed the ingredients in my food, had to be very closely monitored in order to try and manage my behaviour. One sip of the wrong orange juice and I was likely to become a serious risk to the UK.

There are studies which have suggested that allowing children under the age of three years old to watch several hours of television a day might be a cause which contributes to ADHD issues in later life, these studies are not however conclusive. It is thought that brain chemistry and how messages are carried between neurons by neurotransmitters, have a key role to play in how emotions, organisation and attention are managed in the brain. This is considered to be a brain chemistry matter.

My ADHD infused Gaffe

When I was at Uni, my friends and I visited a re-enactment day at a local castle. Cue me thinking I was 'Captain Environment', because I had finished a year studying Environmental Science. I marched over to a guy selling amber and jet jewellery. "Do you know how jet was formed?" I barked at the man in a very cocky manner. Without waiting for a response, I proceeded to explain. That was when the man stopped me, explaining that he was the head of geology at Northumbria University and he knew precisely how jet was created.

I wanted the world to swallow me up. Needless to say, my friends have been enjoying the re-telling of this tale for the past 25 years.

My blood still runs cold at the thought of this event and the many other examples of similar situations I have got myself involved in.

I am convinced that it is my ADHD that drives this behaviour, and I have had to learn to see it coming and slam on the handbrake.

How does ADHD affect us as individuals?

ADHD is often most easy to see in children, the symptoms are often most extreme in youth and most people with ADHD have the condition from their childhood. Most children have lots of energy and many get bored easily. When children get bored it is not uncommon for them to behave in ways that might be mistaken for ADHD. However, ADHD does not just manifest symptoms in how active a child is or whether they misbehave. There are six primary brain functions which ADHD affects and that children with ADHD commonly struggle with, which are:

- The **FLEXIBILITY** of a child to move from one topic or activity to another.

- The ability to **ORGANISE** their thoughts, ideas and surroundings including keeping to one task at a time until completed. The ability to PLAN ahead and set goals, or ideas for the future.

- **EFFECTIVE MEMORY USE** to absorb, store and recover information given to them.

- Separating **EMOTIONS** and logical reasoning and acting appropriately to the scenario taking place in front of them, despite how they might feel.

- **MANAGING INHIBITIONS** after thinking and processing a scenario and then considering the effects that their reactions may have on the scenario.

Many people with ADHD struggle to manage all of the above, however, as with most mental health conditions it may not be that any one person struggles with the same list of factors. Nor might they experience them in the same way. It may be that they recognise some of the traits from their childhood and in adulthood they no longer experience them all.

Whether you are an adult or a child with ADHD, the impact of the condition can be far reaching. This is especially the case if the diagnosis is not established until later in life. Instead, as children these people are often seen as rude, naughty or academically flawed. They often fail to fit in at school and with social groups. Children with ADHD can often find themselves failing to take the time to understand the risks that certain behaviours and actions may pose to them.

The effect of ADHD upon an adult may lead to impulsive behaviour, which can land them in trouble. They may have difficulties maintaining relationships in partnerships and friendship groups. They may not achieve their academic or occupational potential. They may even find it difficult to undertake tasks such as shopping or domestic activities in the home. People with ADHD often act impulsively, which may mean that they make reckless purchases, drive erratically, or behave inappropriately in the workplace; all of which can have serious consequences. I have learned to manage how my ADHD affects me for the most part, although it does tend to be worse when I am suffering with stress or anxiety.

How can ADHD affect those around us?

Parents of children with hyperactivity encounter a range of difficulties because of the effects of the condition. Children with ADHD can be physically and mentally exhausting to live with. As the condition is very often linked to genetics it is not uncommon for parents to suffer with similar symptoms. This may mean that they understand and can help to manage the scenario, or mean that the two antagonise each other and the issues are made worse. It can be very difficult for parents to get support from schools etc., without a proper diagnosis, which can be difficult to get in some instances. Parents can also suffer with both anger and guilt: anger for the combination of factors above and because they might see the behaviour as being naughty and guilt that they can't do more, or that they feel they may be responsible for the child's behaviour in the first place, either genetically or through failure to properly manage perceived misbehaviour.

The impact that adulthood ADHD can have on friends and partners is also difficult to manage. Adulthood ADHD sometimes makes others feel as though they are unwanted, forgotten and overlooked, especially if they think their thoughts and ideas are not taken on board. Partners and family members often feel stressed and exhausted, this can lead to anger and upset. In many instances non-ADHD partners take control of a large proportion of the responsibilities associated with the home and family. This whole scenario can be extremely draining, especially if the same issue arises repeatedly over long periods of a relationship.

I once invited some friends round for dinner and drinks. On my way back from fetching something from the kitchen, I remembered I needed to get something from the bedroom. I went in, got what I needed, but while in there my drink and ADHD addled mind thought, "wouldn't it be nice to lay down for a second on the bed". The next thing I knew, it was morning! My wife was justifiably cross that I had disappeared to bed without warning since nobody knew where I had gone. Luckily, these were very close friends who knew I had a habit of doing unusual things on a whim, so they were not offended. However, it was a pretty rude thing to have done. At the time I could not understand quite why it was rude; I just fell asleep, but after it was explained I got it and have never done it since.

See (NEWS bulletin #10 (June 2024)) in Chapter 24 for an example which demonstrates the value of an ADHD diagnosis in everyday life.

What are the symptoms associated with ADHD?

ADHD symptoms can be split into two main categories; Inattentiveness (difficulty concentrating and focusing) and Hyperactivity/Impulsiveness.

Like most people who deal with ADHD, I often have issues associated with inattentiveness & difficulty with concentrating.

Common issues that this can cause include:

- A limited attention span and being easily distracted
- Making careless mistakes, particularly in academic studies
- Being forgetful or misplacing things
- Struggling to find things when they are not where the person expects to find them
- Seeming to struggle to listen to or carry out instruction
- Being unable to stick to tasks that are tedious or time-consuming (like writing a book – just saying)
- Struggling to organise and prioritise tasks
- Regularly switching between tasks, often leaving tasks incomplete
- Hyperactivity and impulsiveness are also traits which can be expected in someone who is dealing with ADHD examples of this include:
- Fidgeting and being unable to sit still, especially in calm or quiet surroundings
- Struggling to concentrate on tasks
- Talking excessively even in scenarios that they know they should not
- Impatience when waiting for their turn

- Acting without forethought
- Regularly interrupting people speaking
- Taking risks and/or no sense of danger

Complete the tasks you start

I have a habit of being very passionate, maybe even obsessive, about an activity for a few months and then I move on to something else. This is a common trait of people with ADHD. My passion for this book writing project is such that I have been able to maintain my focus on it over the past year. A method I have started to use with projects that I must finish is to remain accountable to them. I have been setting myself regular deadlines for certain aspects of the work and I have been open with a handful of people about what stage I am at with it. This means I need to remain on top of the tasks, as I don't want to let them down when they have been so supportive. When I have had breakdowns, my willingness to be accountable and honest about how I am feeling has been affected, so being made accountable to others is a big driver for me getting across the finish line.

ADHS not ADHD – it's a superpower not a disorder

I believe I have suffered from depression in some form or another since I was a child. I have also dealt with ADHD all my life, although I did not receive an official diagnosis until I was in my early thirties. ADHD was not something I had ever given much thought to until that time and I have never let it hold me back. In fact, if anything, it has been one of my strengths.

Back in March 2023, I heard Paris Hilton interviewed on the Radio. I had previously made many assumptions about Paris, based on very limited knowledge and how the media portrayed her.

Listening to her story, I realised how wrong I was. Paris explained that she had ADHD and that, like me, it was undiagnosed for many years. Everything changed for her once she identified it because it helped her understand more about how she had lived her life. She now treats her ADHD as her 'superpower'.

I am a hundred percent on board with this, as it is one of mine too. ADHD is the part of my manner and personality, which does not like to accept the 'realities' that other people conform to.

When I am told that something I feel very enthusiastic about is not an option, it is my ADHD which propels me to find a way to make it possible; it is the ADHD that turns this into an obsession. As I have developed, I have learned ways to use it that are less abrasive and less aggressive. Combining this with my social and communication skills, I can open doors which other people seem unable to.

People often describe individuals with this ability as disruptors, lateral thinkers who do not always go with the flow or follow social norms. I try not to cause upset or get people into trouble when I do this, as this goes against everything I am about.

From a young age, I learned to believe in the saying 'If you don't ask, you don't get,' which has given me the opportunity to experience some exciting situations.

A good example of this led to me getting my charity beard-shave executed live on the Chris Evans Breakfast Show in the Virgin Radio studios in London, rather than on a chair in a field at CarFest, as initially planned!

It is the same part of me that successfully fought for a promotion on behalf of somebody else, because they deserved it. The part of me that will always defend someone vulnerable caught in a horrible bullying scenario, even if I don't know them.

It's like an unstoppable passion. To be honest, it has occasionally got me into some trouble, but so far, I have always managed to manoeuvre my way out somehow!

How can you help someone to manage their ADHD?

There are all sorts of ways that someone can help a person to manage their ADHD, however many of them involve creating practices and routines which become regular in everyday life. This approach adds structure and a degree of certainty and control to the day. The kind of routines that are easy to include are structured mealtimes, regular exercise, agreed periods of screen time and game times (particularly in children).

Clutter control and specific item storage locations (such as key hooks, coin dishes etc.). are an extension of the support mentioned above and they help to provide further structure to your life. Working to manage storage as well as hobbies and interests etc. can help. Well labelled storage containers, in a well structured storage system is a great place to start. I have found that when new structures are introduced, their regular use in the short term is an important part of remembering to use them long term. Including the person with ADHD in the process of setting up these systems is also a good idea as their input tailors the system to their needs.

Helping someone manage their day with routine can be very useful. This might be done by encouraging them to enter alarms or reminders in a smart phone, or by posting messages around the home and workplace. Regular practice often becomes habitual behaviour when maintained. I have an alarm on my phone every Monday morning to remind me to take milk into the office for the team. I never forget anymore, but the regular reminders are the reason behind this. This is one of many examples.

Giving people with ADHD the space, training and the tools to be mindful, to clear their minds of obligation and be able to enjoy who they are where they is very important and often overlooked. Examples of such tools and practices include activities like art, listening to music, meditation, exercise and cookery. These are all activities which provide distraction and interest.

I appreciate that this is much easier said than done, particularly in adults as we all have busy lives and it can be difficult to eradicate distraction. Having said that, every little helps, so do what you can.

What help is out there?

As with most health issues, it is always wise to start by going to see your GP. I appreciate that in modern times that this may not always be a swift solution, as GP waiting lists can be lengthy, but please don't let this put you off. Get your name on the list and start the ball rolling. The sooner you do this, the sooner the appointment will arrive.

Both therapy and medicinal options may be available by visiting a GP. ADHD can be treated using both methods, but it is thought that a combination of the two approaches is often best.

Treatment is generally arranged by a paediatrician (for children) or psychiatrist; however this is usually in conjunction with support from your GP. If you are concerned over the levels of progress following interaction with your GP, you might need to get a little forceful. In the past I have had to explain that the matter has been going on for a long time and nothing has worked so far and I have requested to be referred to a specialist.

Cognitive Behavioural Therapy (CBT)

CBT is normally carried out in a group, although it can be carried out with a therapist one on one. CBT is designed to work by helping to alter the thought processes that a person has historically used and to build in coping mechanisms, to remind them to find different more effective ways of managing feelings and ultimately a person's approach to a scenario (this works in a very similar way to the milk alarm I mentioned earlier). Again, through practice it is possible to change habits and help a person manage difficult scenarios more effectively for their condition.

ADHD and crappy food

I have already mentioned that, as a kid I was always referred to by family members and doctors as being "hyperactive". Back in those days foods, sweets and drinks were full of vibrant colours which were created artificially. All food additives that have been approved for use by the EU are assigned an 'E' number. If I ate food which contained these additives, I would be bouncing off the walls as a kid. Back in the eighties and nineties, many everyday food manufacturers included these additives as a matter of course; there were just a select few that did not. I could only drink one type of orange juice which did not include the additives that sent me bonkers. Most sweets, or 'goodies' as we called them in Hull, were simply not an option. Not only did these colours and additives cause me to turn into a 'whirling dervish', they fueled my anger and frustration and were the catalyst that helped turn me into a monster for twelve hours. I caused upset to others, but people didn't always realise that I was just as upset.

There were six different additives which we made special efforts to avoid, they were E102 (Tartrazine), E104 (Quinoline yellow), E110 (Sunset yellow FCF), E122 (Carmoisine), E124 (Ponceau 4R) and E129 (Allura red)

Although I think that they may still be used, manufacturers have been pushed to use more naturally sourced additives. I have only listed them here to make you aware of them, just in case they have done similar things to you. Or maybe that they have an effect on someone you love?

To a person looking in, who has not struggled with diet related ADHD, I appreciate that this looks like a benign list of food additives on the back of a packet. To me these are words which represent poisons, or toxins. They stole joy from me as a child. They made me unhappy because I could not have the things that other kids could. They even made me unhappy when I was allowed them, because they caused me to do the things I did. They made the people around me unhappy or even frightened of me and they left me with unhappiness when I was left picking up the pieces of the problems that I had caused.

Chapter 14
Grief

What is grief?

Grief is our physical and psychological reaction to the sudden loss of someone or something that we love or have a bond with.

Most commonly associated with the death of a loved one, grief can also arise from other circumstances. Perhaps a close colleague leaving or retiring, a valued neighbour moving away, a child flying the nest or even the aftermath of a large project you have been organising for a long time, such as a wedding.

There is no right or wrong way to grieve

I have learned that there can be a real divide on how grief manifests in different people. It is something I am comfortable sharing my feelings on, although many are not.

When I was about seven years old, my mum gave me some valuable advice after the first person I knew and cared about passed away. Bob was a lovely man and a friend of my grandparents. Given what a handful I was as a child, he was always kind to me and he always took the time to make me feel welcome. When mum told me he had passed away, I was standing in our kitchen at home and I remember feeling very upset. I had no idea what to do or how to respond. Because of the way my young mind worked, I was aware that there was a chance that I could say or do the wrong thing and seem insensitive and I didn't want to react in that way.

I looked up at the big window over the sink and I couldn't help smiling. Even though I was hurting inside, I could not stop smiling. I felt terrible and told my mum I was sorry.

"Don't worry," she said, "It's okay. Everybody reacts to grief differently and there is no wrong way. Anyone who tells you that there is, is wrong."

This lesson has stayed with me ever since. As you would expect, I have been exposed to many instances of grief since then and each time it happens, my mum's advice always come back to me. I have shared this advice with my own kids. I have also observed that, not only does everyone act differently when tragedy strikes, but everyone's interest in tragedy is different. All of which is OK. Everybody has the right to manage tragedy and grief in their own way without judgement by others.

Poems, humour and my Grandparent(s)

I am no poet, but I have written poems. Usually because I am sad that a valued colleague is leaving work and I want them to know that I remember all the little things about our friendship. As with many aspects of my life, I try to use humour as a way to hide that I am experiencing discomfort, particularly pain or 'heartache'.

My poems are more like limericks really and they are no good at all, but they do the job for me. I want to show the person I love them; not like I love my wife or my family, but I love having them in in my life and I am sad that they will no longer be as accessible to me. I am quite good at remaining in touch with people, but as with all things, life gets in the way and 'long distance' friendships do become less intense as time goes on.

One poem I wrote was after the death of my 'little' grandma, Ida Grimes. Grandma and I had a special bond that I find hard to describe. She was my mate. She lived a hundred miles away from where I grew up, so I didn't see her very often, usually only once a month. This distance and inaccessibility were the catalyst for our friendship to be so strong. In my youth, I would stay with her for a week or two during the summer holidays and we would have a lovely time.

She always made a special effort to do things she knew I would enjoy; made me meals she knew I loved, we'd go all over the Pennines on the bus and we played endless amounts of Monopoly in the sunshine.

She had a very unpredictable cat called George. He was 'unhinged' and could be basking in the sun one minute and then without warning he would sink his claws and teeth into you. He had been the runt of the litter and had mutated feet, on each foot he had between seven and ten toes and claws. This did not hinder him at all. In fact, it made him more adept and vicious in catching and killing Lancashire wildlife and taking lumps out of people he took a fleeting dislike to!

Grandma didn't like letting George out as she lived near a busy road and she always worried about him coming to harm. The rest of the family referred to George as "that evil cat" but Grandma would defend him to the hilt, even though he had destroyed most of her soft furnishings and she had clear scars which matched George's dental records on her legs from the many times he had just flipped his lid. As far as Grandma was concerned, he could not put a (huge) foot wrong!

I haven't really thought about it until now, but Grandma defended me in the same way she defended that cat. We were both a bit broken and although we could be vicious, it may not have always been our fault and she was aware of this. Both of us could also be very loving, but neither of us knew how to manage our frustrations. In the end George fell foul of that busy road, but boy oh boy did he have a lovely life with my grandma.

I loved my grandma dearly and I would like to share my terrible poem that I wrote and read at her funeral. You may not appreciate all of it, as it is quite specific, but it helped me to remember her and the special times we spent together and it still does now. I don't read it very often, but when I do it normally makes me cry. I cannot read it out loud without tears.

I'm sharing this here as an example of how it is possible to navigate a difficult situation. You might not see yourself as a poet, I certainly didn't, and still don't. (Although, if this book is published and I include it, I suppose I'll technically become a published poet.) I'm not someone who particularly enjoys poetry, but writing this helped me cope with something I'm not ready to face and don't want to happen. It also gave me a way to express love and care for someone who may not realise just how much they mean to me.

The other thing it shows which is something I have not thought about until now, is the positive impact that you can have on those around you; your friends, your family, your children and grandchildren. Perhaps without even realising it. Wouldn't it be nice if we could all receive a poem about how much someone cares about us? Ultimately, our whole lives are about building our poems with others.

Oh and by the way, grandma called me her "mushy pea" ... and yes, I am blushing!

"A trip to Grandma's meant..."

A trip to grandmas meant:

A massive hug

It meant Woolworths pic n mix with guaranteed spearmint chews

It also meant tiny little cough sweets that packed a punch, but did the job when the pick n mix had run out

It meant a special smell of prunes and pot-pourri

It meant being thrashed at sit-ups and press-ups

It meant a big ORANGE fluffy sheepskin, which got less orange as the years went by, but not less fluffy

It meant body shop soaps in a rack over the bath, which smelt and looked so much like fruit that you had to lick them, only to find that they didn't taste how they smelt and looked.

It meant having someone to stick up for me when playing Risk.

It meant someone to put up with me when cheating at Monopoly

It meant sitting in the sun in summer

And roasting in the living room in winter because the fire was always on high

It meant a walk down to the old chemical works to see sticklebacks

And riverside matchbox car races down the slide at the park

It meant a height competition until I was about eleven, then it meant lots of stooped hugs

It meant being attacked by a cat with too many claws who was always forgiven and the victim was always the guilty party

At Christmas it meant a silver tinsel Christmas tree and amazing mince pies

It meant looking for the rabbit in a peanut

And receiving £2 sellotaped together in each of our crackers, like magic

It meant obligatory games of bingo.

A visit to Grandma's in the summer meant my first trip to MacDonald's

It meant a steam train ride to the circus

And it meant a tour of Granada Studios and Coronation Street

A trip to Grandma's meant sitting for Sunday dinner with my sister and her own cup of gravy

It meant playing hoops on plastic hoopla, as well as Cowboys and Indians and the greatest white suitcase in the world

It meant heaps of Beano's and Dandy's from the lovely Laura Loo

It meant the world's best meat and potato pie

And heavenly roast potatoes, followed by freshly made chocolate cake and a choice of chocolate biscuits

It meant a porch full of cacti that you must not touch.... But it was just too tempting.

It meant a unique family of wooden sausage dogs and sharing the settee with a large stuffed lion and or tiger

And tea from the teas maid, as soon you wake up

It meant the tastiest porridge ever, eaten from a huge Pyrex bowl

It meant pickle forks and apostle teaspoons

Homemade bread, homegrown yogurt and hydrating prunes

It meant knives, forks and spoons, as well as pots and pans, hand painted on the kitchen walls

It meant playing treasure island on the commodore /4

It meant walking through the personalised yellow and white gates of 'Jackida' and looking for frogs under the metal lid in the garden and running through hanging fingers of the tickle tree

It meant sleeping in fold out beds and watching postman pat and doctor snuggles recorded for me for when I visited (And grandma was the only person in the world who knew how to use their video recorder programmer)

It meant the sound and smell of an 80s coffee percolator

It meant Bettaware gadgets that got used and not pushed to the back of the thingamajig drawer

It meant singing along to cassettes of nursery rhymes sung by Smurfs with silly voices

It meant playing pool for hours on end and eating banana sandwiches on brown bread.

It meant mint tea, now my most favourite comfort drink

Or coffee with cream and honey.

It meant sitting on a wooden bench that you could slide up and down on for dinners, which were made into faces with sausage noses and mashed potato hair

It meant having sandwiches passed through the hatch from the kitchen

It meant a wooden elephant with a man balancing on his trunk and a lovely wooden pig.

It meant ticking chickens and fruit that rang to say dinner was ready.

It meant magazine racks full of crossword books

It meant listening to grandma laughing at things she knew she shouldn't really laugh at and then telling me off for coming up with them in the first place

It meant lots of pictures of a pipe smoking man I loved dearly despite never meeting.

It meant being made to feel so loved and wanted that only those who received that love can understand

It meant spending time with my special friend who I will miss so much I can't tell you.

We love you Grandma; we will never forget you or how you have touched the lives of so many people. You will always be my best mate and I will forever be your mushy pea!"

I never met my little grandma's husband, Jack. Sadly, he died before I was born, but I always felt a strange connection with him when I was growing up. My family has told me I am like him in many ways. When he walked into a room, you knew he had arrived and he wore bright and eye-catching clothes. I believe he was affected by depression and there is a possibility that he passed it to me genetically. Back in those days, people, particularly men, did not understand these things and they certainly didn't talk about them. It is for this reason I feel I have a responsibility to step up and be open about my experience. It is also part of what has driven me to write this book; to help people who might feel similarly to know that it's OK not to be OK.

I want to let people know that there are loads and loads of ways they can get help or help themselves.

I had a grandma and grandad on my mum's side too and they were wonderful people; we had many wonderful times together and it would be remiss of me not to mention them and say how much I loved them and how good to me and my family they were.

Grief management

In my line of work, I am exposed to death and grief on a regular basis. Although I empathise and feel for the people dealing with the process, I am very pragmatic and scientific about this subject. I don't know whether this puts me in a better or worse place to offer advice on the subject. After some thought I concluded that if I had a friend who was struggling with grief, I would care for them and I would provide them with advice, in the same way as other mental health support options.

The first thing to acknowledge is that everyone deals with grief in their own way. To do this, we must give ourselves the time and space to process the situation and accept it without trying to explain the reasons for our thoughts and feelings. It is OK to cry; it is an important part of the body's response to grief but there is no crime in not crying either.

Find a way of communicating your feelings about the person you have lost. Write a poem like I did; write them a letter, sing songs you would listen to together, even talk to them out loud. Say all the things you wanted to say to them but never got the chance to say. There is no harm in saying those things now and it could bring you some relief.

All around my home, I have certain trinkets and belongings of people who I cared about and have lost. When I see them, I automatically think of the pleasant times we had together and why those items represent and embody those people to me. I really get a lot from them, but it is important to notice them and not just let them fade into the background. I do appreciate that this approach might not be for everyone. You must do what is right for you. When I see these items and think of the person, they make me smile and I regularly speak out loud to them. To some extent it keeps them alive to me.

Remember that if you are grieving, someone else will be too. You should not be afraid to communicate and share positive memories of why you both miss them. Offer to comfort them and listen to how they are feeling. For the most part, we are communal beings and coming together during times of grief can really help. However, remember that some people prefer to grieve alone. In these instances, all you can do is offer to be there if they need you. If they choose to come to you, it is important that you make yourself available for them as agreed.

Grief does not always appear as we might think. It can catch up with us when we least expect it. Grief can also hit us more than once, for no apparent reason.

Just remember, there is no right or wrong way for grief to affect us. None of it is our fault and it is very important to accept this and be kind to ourselves.

Chapter 15

The menopause

Why is there a chapter on the menopause in this book?

Yes, I am a man and yes, I understand we do not experience the effects of menopause on our bodies. I also appreciate the danger that I put myself in by discussing the subject! That said, I am the person who will put their head above the parapet. The point I wish to make is important and stands to benefit everyone involved in the conversation, so here goes nothing.

For too long, the menopause is a subject that has been swept under the carpet, particularly by men. We have a responsibility to talk about it and to support those around us through the process. After all, there are Pie Eating Women too!

What is the menopause?

The term menopause is an outdated and ineffective one, used to describe the vast array of changes that occur in a woman's body. It was a term coined by French doctors in the early nineteenth Century (most likely men), to describe the condition a woman finds herself in when she has not had a menstrual cycle for a year or more. When the supply of mature eggs in a woman's ovaries decreases and periods become irregular, the production of hormones such as oestrogen and progesterone also decrease.

It is this reduction in hormones which is thought to be behind many of the symptoms of the menopause. For this reason, many women actively pursue Hormone Replacement Therapy (HRT) available on prescription from their doctor.

What is meant by perimenopause?

Perimenopause is the time period during which a woman experiences many of the symptoms associated with the menopause, but their periods have not yet stopped for a year or more.

Usually, the perimenopause starts between eight and ten years before the menopause. This is not an exact science and the symptoms are different in different people. The symptoms can also mirror that of other illnesses or signs of aging, so it really is a minefield for women.

Most women experience the perimenopause in their forties and the menopause in their fifties, but these ages can differ wildly from person to person. Certain illnesses and treatments can also bring on the menopause early. Typically, healthcare providers inform people about this as part of the process they go through, but this is not always the case.

What are the most common symptoms associated with perimenopause and menopause?

A variety of symptoms are associated with the menopause. The most common of these include:
- Hot flushes
- Heart palpitations
- Irregular periods
- Dry skin
- Dry eyes
- Difficulty sleeping and Night sweats
- Vaginal dryness
- Urinary tract infections (UTIs)
- Headaches and migraines
- Pain in the joints and muscles
- Changes to body shape and weight gain
- IBS
- Ringing in the ears
- Low libido
- Mental illness, including anxiety, stress, depression
- Problems with memory
- Brain fog
- Mood swings
- Tooth sensitivity, sore gums and mouth ulcers

I want to speak exclusively to the fellas that are reading this book. Just read that list of symptoms again and have a think about it for a moment.

Would any of you like to spend, on average, seven years of your life experiencing a combination of those issues?

I'm quite happy to raise my hand here and now and say **NO THANKS!** I would also like to go on record as saying that I would rather the people I love, particularly my wife, mum and female friends and relatives, did not have to either. Despite this, most of them will. Some may experience them for less time (which is still too long, if you ask me) and some may experience them for much longer.

Why should we <u>ALL</u> be talking about it?

There seems to be an unwritten rule, which relates to hangovers, that if someone in a partnership suffers from a hangover, their partner will treat them with contempt, blame them entirely and offer no sympathy. When we were younger, my wife and I agreed we would do the opposite. We agreed that if either of us suffered with a hangover, we would help each other and provide support until they felt better. Granted, it didn't happen very often and this agreement may have grown thin quickly if either of us had abused it. But we didn't, so it worked. Obviously, I'm not comparing hangovers to the menopause, but hopefully you appreciate the sentiment.

Our arrangement has continued through our lives, for any ailment or illness we have suffered with and I love my wife now just as much, if not more, than I did back in those days.

I don't want my wife to feel unwell, unhappy, uncomfortable, or any other 'un'. Sadly, the menopause can cause lots of these issues and many more. As with Mental Health, society has created an atmosphere of shame and guilt which is associated with the menopause, to the point where people are afraid to even mention it.

Well, I want to know if my wife is uncomfortable because if there is something I can do to help, I will do it. We all have a responsibility to learn more about the menopause and how it can affect our loved ones, our friends and family. We need to be more understanding of the symptoms when they arise and be more supportive.

Everyone is affected, so everyone should help

Society conveniently seeks to overlook that no matter who we are, where we go or what we do, the menopause will have an impact on us at some point. If we are married; have female relatives or friends; have female colleagues. Even if we have none of these, we may have relationships with men who have mums/wives/sisters/partners who are going through the menopause.

To properly help, men and women need to work together.

As with most conundrums faced by us humans the most effective way of creating change is through honesty and effective communication. We all need to do our best not to cause or to take offence. We are all on the same side, after all.

We men need to open our minds and our ears and be prepared to talk about the menopause. We need to ask the beloved ladies in our lives to talk to us about it; to tell us how it affects them. If they are having any success with medication, herbal remedies or exercise, could they please let us know. If they are not, how can we support them? We have no right to begrudge or be upset by the actions of people who are suffering. If we try to help them, we reduce the reasons they may become frustrated with us. We need to teach our kids the same lessons, so that they understand as well.

Also, remember that the menopause and anything to do with the female menstrual cycle can often be a taboo subject even for women, even more so within certain faiths and with people from different cultural backgrounds. Because of this, many women feel under-educated on the subject. I have heard awful stories about women seeking support from their GP as they did not know what was happening to their bodies, or when they could not get support from those around them, plucking up courage to get medical advice only to be met by a male doctor who did not know enough to offer any advice.

We also need to ask all the women in our lives to be open with us and reassure them that when the time comes, we will love them and support them no matter what. We must encourage them to communicate with us about how they are feeling.

Below are a handful of things I picked up on at a recent talk that I attended by menopause specialist Dr Louise Newson. The conversation was about the advice she offered to women who have concerns over the menopause and its effects.

First, she suggested women download her 'Balance' App. It is an app which contains useful help and advice for managing menopausal symptoms. Vitally, it also contains a questionnaire which women can use to monitor their symptoms, which can then produce a health report which they can present to a health professional to guide them with any help that they can offer. As there are no diagnostic tests which can measure the perimenopause or the menopause, monitoring the symptoms is a vital step.

She advised women to better educate themselves about perimenopause, the menopause and management options. We should all do this, not just women. Most employers offer courses on these subjects and if they don't it's our responsibility to enquire about having them made available.

Medical professionals can prescribe hormones or HRT. Depending on the symptoms, these prescriptions may assist with the difficulties of these conditions. Dr Newson also advised against the use of compounded hormones without first seeking medical advice, as they can be expensive and are not regulated, which can cause complications.

Diet can also play a part; it is worth researching things that women could include in their diets to help to manage symptoms. Whole foods such as fresh fruit and vegetables, high-quality proteins; omega three sources, like nuts and oily fish; phytoestrogen, which is found in foods like soya and oats, all have the potential to assist with the symptoms of the menopause.

Exercise helps too. It might be less appropriate to do high-intensity exercise, but weight and resistance training can be helpful, along with Yoga and Pilates for some women. These are things men can also get involved with if our friends and loved ones are uncomfortable going on their own. Everyone is different, though and maybe what works for one may not work for someone else. That's when we really can come into play, by being there to listen and support. Or being willing to change our diets to something that might benefit our loved ones so that they are not alone.

'Teamwork makes the dream work'.

To sum up, there are many things that can help. But removing all stigma or shame from the process is very important, making it easier for everyone.

NOTE: I thought long and hard about whether to include this chapter. After removing it and reinstating it twice, I decided to go ahead. Fingers crossed it was the correct decision!

Chapter 16
Maintaining good mental health

My mental health is my problem

The mental health conditions we have been looking at are not like an infection; something that hits us hard and drops us to our knees overnight and we recover from after a week or so. My mental health conditions are part of my being. In learning to live with them, I have found that many things can affect them. How well I manage them on a day-to-day basis has a direct impact on how I respond to the circumstances that life throws at me.

Although I am very passionate about helping others with their mental health, it is not always possible and it is a common misconception particularly of those who are suffering with their mental health, that the world has a responsibility to provide that person with the feedback that they wish to hear.

Our mental health and wellbeing are our own responsibility; anything beyond that is a welcome gift from others. While I encourage everyone to be kind to one another, kindness can sometimes involve delivering honest truths that a person may not want to hear. This is especially true for those of us in roles where such conversations are part of the job.

My mental health is also often affected by the scenarios that the people around me find themselves in and how I respond to them.

My ability to recognise triggers and how well I am able to manage how I respond to those triggers is usually affected by how well I am looking after myself.

When I am calm, well rested and have been eating the right things in the right amounts, I am far more in control of things. And far more capable of seeing the things that are headed my way. This is particularly the case in work; the more frantic and disorganised I get the more likely things are to cause me to fail. This affects my ability to manage the tasks at hand and also my ability to step back and see the bigger picture.

When I am needed to be at my best because of the number of plates I am trying to spin, I can get bogged down and struggle to even get my head around the basics.

Managing mental health is a journey, not an action

I never consider myself to be recovered from depression. It is a condition I will have and will manage all my life. The way it affects me is as much down to me as it is to anything else. I rely upon my loved ones being brutally honest with me from time to time, telling me when they see that my actions and behaviours are not as they should be. I have also had to make some difficult decisions about the things I am prepared to expose myself to, to avoid becoming triggered.

My point is, it's always there, it never goes away. I have better periods and less than better periods and that's OK.

Managing our mental health and preventing things from getting out of control can be tough. There are lots of little things in our everyday lives that niggle us. On their own, the likelihood of them causing us to go into freefall is minimal and for this reason, we often overlook them.

As these things add up, they become a set of problems which can do as much harm as one bigger problem might; but because they sneak up on us they are harder to notice. Add larger problems into the mix, the things in work and home life which are out of our control and these tiny issues have the potential to be the straw that breaks the camel's back.

I have found it useful to take advantage of 'easy wins' as part of my method for managing these issues and building in mental health resilience.

Throughout this book I have tried to share easy wins and routine-based methods and practices that have helped me. They were all an important part of my recovery, so you might find that they help you too.

Don't make money your priority

People regularly use social media to advertise their life coaching services. Nine times out of ten, these people seem to encourage us to 'change your life', 'earn six figures a year', 'refuse to settle for a normal life', 'show those who doubted you' and so on. They seem to want to take people and encourage them to become something else, to leave their life behind and earn a fortune!

Of all the people I speak to, I don't know anyone who says that money brings happiness. Having money brings choices and allows people to do things they may not have been able to otherwise, but it does not create happiness and it is very dangerous to believe that it does.

Without a person being comfortable with who they are, with or without wealth, without a person understanding their needs, their mental state and how they can be well, wealth is ultimately irrelevant.

I have a very good friend who works with several exceedingly wealthy people. They told me that of all the people they have met, only two of them are truly happy with themselves and their lives.

If you are thinking of working with a life coach, first take the time to consider their motives. People who will share the benefit of their experience at no cost and who have nothing to gain from you are the people most worth listening to and confiding in.

Wealth provides opportunities, it can give people choices and it can help people to simplify their lives.

You can find emotional wealth regardless of whether you have financial wealth or not. It may sound like a cliché, but I promise it's true (I am proof of this).

Honesty

Maintaining our mental health requires us to be in touch with many aspects of our lives, starting with our thoughts and our physical health; but more than anything, it requires us to be honest with ourselves and those around us. Knowing our frailties and our strengths and embracing both is vital to help us move forward.

The first step on this journey requires us, or you in this case, to be fully honest with yourself and me. I rarely come across anyone entirely satisfied with every aspect of their life or who feels there isn't an element of their life that bothers them at least a little, or even a lot.

We all have times in our lives when we have had secrets, worries and concerns for our health or for our future. To get maximum benefit from reading this book, it will be helpful to acknowledge some of those difficulties - sooner rather than later, if you can. Doing so will be very beneficial for you. I believe that recognising and acknowledging our flaws, whether they be mental health, behaviours or mistakes we have made is the source of all future betterment.

I have included a worksheet for your use in Chapter 25. You can use this worksheet to make notes on the elements of your life you may wish to consider as part of this process.

WARNING, THIS PROCESS CAN BE EMOTIONALLY DRAINING AND MAY BE DISTRESSING, SO PLEASE GO STEADY. YOU MAY WISH TO KEEP THIS ASPECT PRIVATE TO START WITH.

If we know where we went wrong, even better how or why, we might just be able to avoid doing it again and take something from that scenario that helps us learn from it. It may even turn into a massive positive. We cannot undo the past. We can only make the best of the scenario that exists now.

Facing up to this stuff is one of the most difficult steps in this process; life does not come with a manual and even if it did, there would have to be a different one for every one of us. We are all unique and that one person may have absolutely no concerns about could be something that eats away at you every hour of every day.

The way I like to look at this is to ask - Am I feeling OK?

If the answer is no, or I'm not sure, or even if you had to think before pressing yes, you might just want to think about having a chat with someone.

Asking for help

Little things add up; a computer not working, getting caught up in a road rage incident, a rude shop assistant, forgetting about a minor job you needed to do. There is almost always a way to manage these things and circumnavigate the negatives they create. Either they get done and you put the problem to bed, or you discover an alternative solution. Whatever happens carrying with you the blame, or the frustration which arose because of it, is a total waste of time and energy. At worst simply acknowledge it happened, accept that in future the scenario can be dealt with differently and move on. When you come to the section on meditation (Chapter 19), this is precisely what this activity teaches us to do.

There's no such thing as a bad idea

I am a lateral thinker and I believe there is no such thing as a bad idea. In fact, the crazier the idea, the better! Even if an idea seems crazy and not a solution at all, there might be a chink of light within it. Something that we can nurture and encourage to become an amazing idea or a perfect solution.

My wife says, "If you throw enough shit at a wall, some of it will stick" and she is so right.

Another great way to solve a problem is to ask a kid. Kids are geniuses; their minds are so young and free that they will look at a situation from a totally different viewpoint than you or I ever would! Because we are grown-up!

Seeking support from a counsellor or a talking therapist

A counsellor is someone who makes time to sit and speak with us on a one-to-one basis about the obstacles we are facing in our life.

We can openly talk about our feelings and emotions without worrying about being judged. They help us gain a greater understanding of how our feelings may connect with other elements of our life and our past. The aim is to help us find our own solutions or coping mechanisms for managing our scenario. They do this without advising or telling people what to do, but by coaching us and guiding us towards our own solutions.

The importance of happiness

The Harvard study of adult development has shown that happiness is a significantly influential factor in helping people thrive and be significantly less stressed.

The study, which began in 1938, has demonstrated that a key factor in people's happiness is being part of a companionship. It found that those who cultivate positive and strong relationships with other people experience greater long-term happiness and health. This has proved to be the most significant way to reduce stress and improve happiness levels.

Working from home

Ever since the outbreak of the Covid-19 virus turned the world upside down in 2019/2020, many people now work from home. This suits some people and not others. For those who find these arrangements a challenge, it may be useful to treat working from home similarly to working from the office, where possible. Get up, wear a regular work outfit. This provides a division between home life and work life, allowing your mind to do the same. I am lucky to have an office at home. I have made it as pleasant as possible by decorating it and putting up pictures that I love. I find it useful to close the door to the office when I finish work each day and over the weekend. It leaves work in that room and the rest of my home remains my home. I appreciate that this option isn't available to everyone, but it is important to make your workspace as comfortable as possible and to try and have a way of putting it away when you are not using it, even if that takes a bit of time each day. I used to use a bureau and that was quite good too. It was tall with shelves above the fold out bit, so I could store my printer, laptop and paperwork in there. Most importantly it was easy to put away each evening. This mattered as it was in my living room.

Take regular breaks from your desk

When you are working from home, it is very tempting not to take regular breaks, or to work through your lunch break. I have found that taking a break freshens up my mind. Even going to the kitchen to make a cuppa or having a wander and looking out of the window. At lunchtime, go for a short walk or do some exercise; like push ups or jogging on the spot. Get the blood flowing round your body. Boosting the oxygen in your bloodstream will increase your attention levels, helping you to feel happier and boosting your productivity!

Keeping a stress journal

By keeping a journal of situations which put you under stress, you can monitor many aspects of what you notice about how you are feeling when you become stressed. Include information such as:

- the date of the event
- the time
- the location of the event
- the task that was being undertaken at the time
- who you were with (if anybody)
- whether you were aware of precisely what had caused you to feel stressed
- a description of how the situation made you feel, both physically and emotionally

- a brief description of the scenario and what happened
- a stress rating from one to ten for before the event
- a stress rating from one to ten during the event
- a stress rating from one to ten after the event
- how long the feeling of stress lasted

The value of the journal is that it helps you become more aware of the circumstances that cause you stress. They help to identify patterns that occur over time, to recognise whether there may be a biological or chemical influence, whether certain foods cause problems or whether there are specific triggers which cause you stress and whether particular activities, or people or a combination of the two increase your level of stress.

Establishing these things can help you to manage your feelings moving forward. They help you to anticipate and positively prepare yourself for a situation before it occurs, so that you can either avoid it, or better manage it to reduce the negative impacts of stress upon you. Other important methods of stress management can include:

- Making time to relax and be mindful. This might include taking up a hobby, sport, meditation or simply walking the dog. The important thing is to create a space to be away from life's stressful situations.
- Choose not to get frustrated or angry about anything you cannot influence. 'Pick your battles', as my boss always says. Being unable to influence a scenario you feel

strongly about can be very upsetting and will raise stress levels. Learning to do this is possible, I know because I have been developing the skill over the past fifteen years. It is difficult and it requires a lot of self-awareness. I find writing my thoughts down and refining them until I decide whether there is still a need for me to say them out loud is a useful technique.

- Be grateful for the positive things in life and try not to dwell on the negatives, or the things that didn't go well. Use these as a learning tool to avoid being exposed to the same thing again in the future.
- Try to be organised. Do not look at a list of problems as one large amorphic problem. Instead, break the big stuff into lots of smaller bites and deal with one thing at a time. As the list of problems reduces, things feel less oppressive and we have greater control.
- Try to eat well and exercise regularly. Good gut health and exercise, particularly outdoor exercise, improve mental health and reduce stress in most people. This is something I absolutely have not mastered and must work on.
- Just one hour spent walking in a green space reduces fight-or-flight reactions, such as stress and anxiety, significantly.

Be kind to yourself - learn to say no

We are all busy people. Modern life is busy. Visiting friends and family, going to work, walking the dog, trips to the cinema. We volunteer, water the garden; the list is endless.

On top of all that, many of us agree to do things for other people. We agree to help them out with this and that. We agree to all-sorts of things and if we are not careful, our lives become so busy, there is not enough time to do the things we need to do. Nor is there enough time for us to take some space for ourselves, to be mindful, to enjoy our hobbies, or even just to rest and recharge.

We need to master the skill of saying no. Knowing when and how to say no is not easy. We often feel we are letting someone down.

You may remember that in Chapter 7, I said that whether you like it or not; you are the most important person in your life. We may well be nine chapters on, but this still remains the truth. If you do not take care of yourself, you cannot help others. Learning to honour this and say no helps to provide us with control over our schedule, helping to protect against other people's demands on our time.

One way of doing this is to set some time aside each week, some sacred time. Under no circumstances let people book you during those times.

Here's an example. Every Tuesday evening, I meet with friends at a local cafe to play board games. To some people, playing board games might seem childish, but I find it to be very good for my mental health. I have become very close friends with the group I play with and we can talk about things which we would not be comfortable discussing in front of just anyone. If other people try to make plans for me on a Tuesday, I say that I can't make it as I am attending 'Nerd Night'.

Golden rule - never compare yourself with others

My golden rule is not to worry about what other people think, have, or do. Make the best of what you have. Life is not a contest and those who see it this way are missing out. Write your own story; do not waste time wishing you were someone else, simply be who you would like to be.

You are awesome!

Social media and more traditional media forms, such as TV and magazines, are very toxic drivers for this desire to be like someone else. Influencers and media personalities like to be seen wearing designer brands, or are being paid to promote them.

The friends and acquaintances that appear as we scroll through our social media threads can encourage us to believe that they live lives that are superior or more glamourous when compared to ours; bigger houses, more expensive cars or holidays we could never afford. What we all need to remember is that most people, famous or not, want to present their best side to the world. They like to be seen wearing their best clothes and living their best lives and on top of all that, they add fake filters to make everything look even shinier!

Every snapshot of someone's seemingly perfect or exciting life reflects one moment in time, but with these moments of hundreds of different people constantly popping up on our feed, can feel like everyone is doing something wonderful all the time, when in fact this is not the case.

You do not need to worry if you do not have the high-flying business that your old mate from school has. But it is still important to occasionally ask yourself "Am I happy?"

If the answer is yes, there is no problem. However, if the answer is no, think about what would make the difference and how you can achieve this. You should ensure that you base this on your own dreams and ambitions and not someone else's. See chapter 20 for my take on bucket lists and how important I think they are. Here are some things that I do for you to consider, to help you live your life your way:

- Wear comfortable clothes no matter how they look.
- Wear the fashion you prefer, not just what your peers wear.
- Sing in public if it brings you joy.

- Talk to your dog on a walk if that makes you feel happy.

Channel your 'inner Anthony Hopkins' (see Chapter 10)

Get to a place where you are not concerned with what other people think as long as you are happy and not harming anyone else.

Big G's Campaign for Positivity on Facebook

All this, along with the hostility that exists on social media, led me to set up a Facebook group called 'Big G's Campaign for positivity on Facebook' (snappy title, I know). The group is a safe space to chat and focus on the bright side of life, with only positive posts allowed. No sport or politics! The group now has over two thousand five hundred members and during tough times like the COVID-19 pandemic, members said that it kept them feeling involved. It's a great place to feel happy, supported and stay connected with good people.

Who can you talk to?

This is the million-dollar question. The simple answer is, someone you feel comfortable talking to, someone who will keep the information as safe as you need it to be. Someone you feel will offer you the type of support you need from them, which can differ from person to person.

Here are some suggestions of people you could talk to:

- People you know, friends, family members, colleagues.

- Healthcare professionals, your GP, mental health support workers and specialists.
- Charity representatives and volunteers.
- Support groups offering regular support which can be specific to your needs, like 'Men's Sheds', 'Andy's Man Club' or addiction support groups.
- Your employers or health professionals connected with your employers.

Alternatively, there are groups not specifically designed for mental health support which bring people together from all walks of life. Under different circumstances the members might not normally come together. I have found these groups and clubs to be an excellent resource for my own support and a safe place for healthy discussions.

Examples of these include meditation classes, yoga classes, board game groups and sports teams, to name just a few.

The list is endless and it does primarily depend on what you are comfortable with, but it is worth considering. Talking to someone or doing something that might normally be outside of our comfort zone is something we need to do if we want things to change.

If you haven't already noticed, one of the key themes of this book is about redefining our comfort zone and discovering if there are any new or different ways to approach a situation.

Mental health can fluctuate

Nowadays, I am well most of the time, however my mental health still fluctuates. I do everything I can to manage this. The first thing I do is notice that I am not feeling quite right. That might sound obvious, but sometimes it's not. It is nothing to worry about; there could be lots of reasons for this. However, if this happening more and more, it might be something you need to consider taking professional advice about.

Once I notice that something isn't quite right, I try to think about the past few days and whether I have been doing anything out of the ordinary which might have affected the status quo.

Ultimately, nobody knows you better than you. You are the best person to write your own questions to establish if changes have occurred. I would suggest that you still consider some of the above questions though, as they are common causes. It might also be useful to ask those close to you if they have noticed any change indicators in you. It was my wife who spotted that I get grumpy when I'm hungry. I had never noticed this. You may find that you have been overlooking some of your indicators.

List of Change Indicators

	Have I had too much sleep?	Y/N
	Have I had enough sleep?	Y/N
	Have I eaten enough healthy food?	Y/N
	Has my diet changed? How?	Y/N
	Am I hungry?	Y/N
	Am I thirsty?	Y/N
	Am I unwell?	Y/N
	Has the weather changed? (hot/cold?)	Y/N
	Have I taken medication?	Y/N
	Have I had alcohol?	Y/N
	Have I used recreational drugs?	Y/N

A blank version of this form is available for your use in Chapter 25.

It is also sensible to discuss your concerns with someone you trust. Someone that knows you well, particularly if you spend time with them regularly. They are likely to notice if you have been acting any differently. They can also keep an eye out for any changes from that point onwards and keep you informed.

It may also be worth a trip to the doctor, especially if you are already using meds to help manage your mental health. They are the best people to decide whether you need to make changes to the medication you are taking, or if you need something different.

Usually, when my equilibrium is 'out of whack' it is because I have forgotten to take my meds; I have not drunk enough; or because I have not had enough sleep. The symptoms I experience when I haven't had my meds are recognisable, which is helpful. I go a little dizzy and my eyes feel like they are wobbly in my skull.

If it is one of the other scenarios, then I may feel tearful, not like I'm going to burst into tears, but I if I were to watch the end of E.T. I could.

We have talked about being present and mindful already and this is an excellent example of why this is so important. Being aware of your senses, aware of who you are and how you feel and listening to that, is a vital element of your own Mental Health Management. Failing to be aware of these issues can be quite a slippery slope and things can go downhill incredibly quickly.

Again, maintaining a dialogue with those around you about how you feel and any concerns you have will help them support you and to be understanding when times are hard.

If you think nothing has changed, to make you feel this way, monitor yourself as it may mean that you should visit your GP again and discuss the problems that you are experiencing. They may offer an alternative solution.

Chapter 17
The value of healthy routines in recovery

Routine is key

During my breakdowns and difficult periods, I found it was easy to let routines slip. Getting up at the same time each day, washing and getting ready to go out, even if I wasn't going anywhere, really worked for me. Some days, I felt like I could not even get out of bed.

So make it your priority to,

Get up!! Get dressed!! Go out!! and do!!

This comes up regularly when I am helping other people with their mental health. Most people I speak to who are starting to feel better agree that routine becomes extremely important and is a helpful tool for them to rely on, particularly on days when they feel they are having a bit of a wobble.

The small steps we take as we recover often feel as though we are not getting anywhere, even when we are. Recovery can feel painfully slow.

Here's a way to recognise the progress that you are making; each night, before going to sleep, identify three things that you have achieved that day. It doesn't matter how small you feel those things are, either write them down or make a note of them on the calendar on your phone. Soon you will have a record showing that you are moving forward and gaining strength and confidence every day.

A motivating factor during my difficulties was to make the decision that depression had already stolen enough from me and I would not allow it to steal my future dreams and ambitions as well. By doing all we can to think this way and seek to overcome the monster that is mental ill health, we give ourselves something to fight for.

Get up earlier

Set your alarm for fifteen minutes earlier than normal two or three times a week and try to be strict about getting up. That extra fifteen minutes is unbelievably valuable and will help you feel more organised. Furthermore, you will have more time in the morning before you need to get on with your day. Why not stop, sit down, enjoy a calm cup of tea and find yourself?

Fifteen minutes a day, three days a week, fifty-two weeks a year is more than an extra day and a half! Thirty-nine hours per year to yourself, to do with whatever you please.

Apparently, if you struggle to sleep at the right time, you should try setting your alarm and getting up thirty minutes before you would normally wake up. This resets your body clock and should allow you to start a new sleep routine. I have done this and it has worked. Give it a go if this is an issue for you.

Get up early and go somewhere exciting

Get up early on a Sunday morning; go somewhere and cook breakfast on a camping stove or BBQ in the countryside or go for a paddle in the sea or a stream. Do things that are not run of the mill and make for an exciting change. Take your family or meet a friend. It really is a lovely thing to do.

Make your bed

Start your day by making your bed. This is a positive psychological statement. It draws a line under the overnight period of rest and leaves your room in a tidy state. It also means that no matter how difficult, or how long your day might have been, when you are ready to go to bed, you will find your bed organised, comfortable and prepared for you to go to sleep. This may not seem like much, but it is showing the day you mean business; you have completed a task and you have only just got started!

Wash up or empty the dishwasher

For me, washing up or loading and emptying the dishwasher is the ultimate, quick problem solver. You start with a problem, a heap of messy pots and in around five minutes, you have a solution; clean pots washed and/or put away, without too much mental input and the dirty ones in the dishwasher ready to go when full.

The other thing about this task is that it is a fast win! Say you have a list of jobs that need doing, but you cannot decide which to tackle first. Starting with the washing up leads to the pots being put away, then I wipe down the kitchen sides and this leads to a bit of tidying up. This might then lead to me putting some stuff away elsewhere in the house. While I do that, I may see that another job that needs attention.

Once things are tidy, I can choose to hoover and clean the floor. If I am hoovering the kitchen, I may as well do the rest of the ground floor and so on.

Can you see how one job leads to another? So, if in doubt, just wash up!

Make your own lunch

This is another mindful process. Take the time to make your own lunch and include the things you like. Maybe you are managing your diet for health reasons, trying to manage your weight, or to improve your sleep routines. Like many people, I have lived my life on a budget and making your own lunch can be an excellent way of managing finances while putting together a meal that you enjoy.

Try something new

When you are out and about, look at the signs and adverts on the noticeboards in church yards, sports centres, or supermarkets; not only can this be quite an interesting and mindful activity, but there may also be resources that are of use to you there. There are all kinds of interesting clubs and activity groups out there where like-minded people come together and do stuff. Anything from groups who get together and play board games, to woodwork classes. It is an opportunity to try activities and groups that you might otherwise have never thought of trying.

> **Switch out bad choices for good ones**
>
> Try new things, find healthier options that you really love and use them to replace something in your life which you know to be less healthy. It's all about compromise.
>
> I recently discovered some flavoured sparkling water drinks by a company called Dalston's. They make soft drinks that contain no added sugar so they are not too sweet. They're a refreshing, mature alternative to alcohol and I now choose to drink Dalston's over beer on a sunny afternoon, or when I want to chill out.
>
> Dalton's also make a wide range of gut healthy drinks too. There are links between good gut health and good mental health (before you ask I am not sponsored by them, I just love their drinks as an alternative to alcohol).

Eat socially

When you entertain friends and family, have meals which involve getting hands on. Create meals with lots of dishes on the table that people spoon from, or tear and share. The physical sharing of food is such a social and involved way of being with those you care about. Sharing and eating food this way breaks down barriers and encourages conversation much more easily than a meal served on a plate to each person individually. Get hands on, get in there.

Being 'present' or 'in the moment' while eating

You can adopt this approach as part of many of your activities. But there is one way that will really help you get into this mindset. Practice this while eating.

Each time you put something in your mouth, provided it isn't too hot and if you are not eating like a gannet (something I have a habit of doing), take time to chew it ten times. While you are doing this, think about the flavours and the textures you are experiencing. Be aware of all elements of the food you are eating and savour the meal as fully as possible.

Listen to music

This one seems obvious to me! Music is a huge part of my life. The thing is, when we struggle with our mental health, sometimes the things that seem obvious when we are feeling well become distorted or overlooked. Listening to a favourite song really can lift your spirits and inspire you. Even better, create a playlist of several songs that make you feel good. If you do this when you feel well, you don't have to think too much about when you need a boost.

I have three songs that are easy for me: "Band on the Run" by Wings (but I also like the cover by the Foo Fighters), "Sunscreen" by Baz Luhrmann (This book is inspired by this song) and "It's not easy being Green" by Kermit the Frog. This song may sound solemn, but it's about accepting who you are and embracing yourself for that.

Music is a personal and emotive thing, so don't be surprised if you come across songs that have the opposite effect of making you feel well; another reason for compiling a list in advance while you are in a better place.

Move your fruit bowl

If you want to eat less junk food and processed snacks and switch to more fruit, you can be brave and try not to buy the junk food. If you find this hard, try putting the fruit bowl in the room you sit in the most. Having easy access to the fruit bowl will make it more convenient and more easily accessible than going to that dastardly snack drawer.

My sock drawer

I hate wearing odd socks, it is a big trigger for me and can affect my entire day. I am not bothered if others wear odd socks - I don't get it, but for me it is important to wear matching socks. To manage this, I have worn the same type of socks since I was a teenager. Despite the company being taken over a few times, the socks have remained the same, even though the brand name has changed.

The only difference has been in the sock's design. There used to be one type, there are now three. They have a 'sports sock' (the ones I've always worn and pretty much pull up to my knees). The 'trainer sock', which are the super short socks that you can't really see when you wear trainers with shorts. And the sneaky 'ankle sock' which is something between the other two.

They used to do them in packs of white socks, packs of grey socks and packs of black. To cut a long story short, I had a sock drawer full of socks of different colours and lengths. It was driving me bonkers!

I would start my day frustrated because finding a comfortable, matching pair of socks was a total bloody nightmare. This went on for months! Until I realised what I was doing to myself.

So, I went to the shop that sells these socks and bought three large packs of them for just over £20. I skipped home and threw away all the socks in my sock drawer, replacing them with eighteen sparkling new, matching pairs of socks.

Now when I go to put on my socks, not only am I not put in a bad mood automatically, but I also actually take great pleasure in taking out a pair of matching socks and putting them on. For the sake of £20 and twenty minutes, I changed something that annoyed me every single day into something that cheers me up every day.

Keep your feet warm and dry

Yes, another feet related one! (My wife says I'm obsessed) This one is self-explanatory. I am rarely more comfortable than when my feet are warm and dry. I do not enjoy having cold feet, or wet shoes and socks at all, it makes me miserable. It is probably another reason I love Egypt so much. My feet are always warm and dry there, at least when I'm above the waves, anyway.

Even in the deepest, darkest winter, if your feet are warm and dry, you will feel cosy. I even have one of those electrical big slippers that my wife bought me for Christmas one year. In the winter when I am working from home, I can keep my feet warm with no need to put the heating on…… Bliss!!

The value of routine in recovery

When things get hard for me, one of the first things I do is abandon my daily routines. It's a bit like I rebel against them; or that the shock of being in difficulty makes me lazy-minded and lethargic, pushing me to avoid routine which I normally find extremely helpful. It's as though I psychologically adopt the foetal position to protect myself.

My friend Capt. Elliot, who is a scuba diving instructor, recently gave me an insight into this through nature. We were scuba diving together and I was pleased to see that coral was being nurtured and grown on man-made structures in the shallows around the island. They were doing this for scientific research on coral recovery.

Coral is incredibly slow growing and hard coral (there are both hard and soft corals) is the slowest. Different species grow at different rates, but some corals can grow as slowly as 1cm per one hundred years. When I looked closely at these underwater structures, I could see the juvenile corals growing and multiplying. Without the structure being put in place and the support of the scientists, this would not happen.

Our recovery from a mental health crisis is a similar process. Just like coral, it only takes one storm; one chemical spill; or one greedy parrot fish to take things back to zero. So, slow and steady wins the race, particularly in the early stages.

For me, routine is the scaffolding on which I build the rest of my life. Just as I have mentioned elsewhere in the book, it is always an opportunity for a new start. There is nothing to stop you from doing the same.

A major step in this is how I start my day. You have probably already guessed that I listen to the Chris Evans Breakfast Show on Virgin Radio every weekday morning. I find the subjects discussed and the wholesome chat that forms the bulk of the show rewarding, especially first thing in the morning. This and events like CarFest, the festival that Chris created, have been beneficial to me and other listeners.

As with my sock story (above) and giving gratitude (see chapter 18), the first things that we do in a morning are incredibly beneficial to our overall wellbeing for the day. So, why wouldn't we do them? I'm not saying that we need to listen to Chris's show, although I might suggest you try it! You might prefer listening to classical music, heavy rock, a podcast, or even birdsong. Just try to do something at the start of your day which will subliminally benefit your wellbeing; before building other beneficial steps into your routine for the rest of the day.

Maintain a healthy sleep routine

Sleep is incredibly valuable for our mental and physical health.

We must include the correct balance of exercise and rest each day. Our intake of caffeine and nicotine in the hours before we go to bed is likely to hinder our ability to have a good night's sleep. Keeping to regular bedtimes and waking up at the same time every morning helps us make sure we get the correct amount of sleep regularly.

I meet people who say they do not sleep well, but they make no effort to change their daily routine. During the day, there are many elements that can interrupt or benefit sleep; not keeping to the same sleep routine every day is one surefire way to mess with your ability to sleep when you need to. We should all aim for eight hours of sleep a night, but the older we get, the harder this can be. The usual suspects which disrupt our sleep patterns include:

- Mental health

- Stress & anxiety levels
- Physical health
- Medication
- Alcohol consumption
- Caffeine consumption
- Using screens before bed
- Daytime sleeping
- Activity carried out during the day
- Body weight
- Diet
- Sugar consumption
- Water consumption
- Light levels
- Temperature
- Mattress suitability

*Caffeine can disrupt our ability to rest and sleep for up to twelve hours!

This is just a small list of the issues that can affect our sleep. What it does highlight is that almost every aspect of our day can affect our quality of sleep.

The pitfalls of the wrong routine

I know that routine also helps me manage some of the negative scenarios that can arise from my ADHD. By sticking to certain routines, I reduce the risk of losing things and I am more organised as I go about my day. When I was recovering from my breakdown, I found it was easy for me to be drawn into bad routines; routines that were a distraction rather than a good management technique.

For instance, I bought lots of flat pack furniture which had to be put together; I decorated rooms, stripped window frames and found jobs in the home which occupied my time beautifully. But also gave me excuses not to look for a job and prevented anyone saying that I had not been productive. This behaviour formed part of my recovery, so it was important. But there was no balance and the routines I was adopting were not long-term routines to help with my recovery, they were short-term tasks designed to convince myself and those around me I was busy and therefore could not go back to work.

Without me realising it, this was increasing my stress and anxiety levels, even though I was out of the toxic bullying scenario.

Chapter 18
Kindness, gratitude and forgiveness

Humankind not Human-unkind

Recently, while watching a TV program about ancient Egypt, I noticed they used the word 'Humankind' repeatedly. So often that it really stood out!

This got me thinking; Humankind refers to all humans! We have a responsibility to live up to the word. If we all try to be Humankind and have understanding by default, it will have an incredibly positive impact on those around us who subscribe to the opposite approach, let's call them part of "Human-unkind."

Kindness

Most of this book is about being kind in one way or another. Whether directed towards ourselves or others, kindness rules for me. One thing is for sure: being unkind rarely causes another person to be kind, whereas kindness may encourage an unkind person to operate differently.

Kindness can appear in many forms and it should really start with us. We must look after and be kind to ourselves. The modern world we live in can be tough sometimes. To give ourselves a fair chance of making the best of things and to put us in a place where we can help others, we need to give ourselves a break.

The British love to support the underdog, but simultaneously are keen to be seen as hard done by. The media love to bash people for being successful and for being proud. I don't think for a moment that you or I, or this book, are likely to change that anytime soon, but there is no reason why we, as individuals, should not be a little more proud of our achievements.

The three states of gratitude and forgiveness

As I was writing about these two words, it came to me that each of these words has three different states and they are all slightly different.

The three states of gratitude

1. You can give gratitude to others;
2. you can have gratitude for the life and things you have;
3. and you can receive gratitude from others.

The three states of forgiveness

1. You may forgive yourself for feelings, scenarios, or mistakes you have made;
2. you can offer forgiveness to someone else;
3. and someone else can forgive you.

Without going too over the top, isn't that wonderful? Stop and think about it for a moment.

With these simple words, which are just sounds made by our throat and mouth, we can feel forgiveness for bad things that have happened, but also thankful for the good things we have. These words can help us and others move past something that has happened, without fear of revenge or lingering guilt.

Of course, I know that context matters and many situations are more complex than just saying a word and considering it resolved. However, it's a good starting point and a worthwhile goal. Using kind words can ease a difficult relationship and show someone that you care about them, value them and want to keep them in your life.

It might take practice, but instead of immediately defending ourselves when something goes wrong, we should try saying, "Sorry." Only say it if you genuinely mean it. If you are truly sorry and willing to make things right, it is the best way to move forward. It is also difficult for someone to argue against an apology. The ability to offer forgiveness and gratitude is a gift more valuable than any wealth and if you practise them regularly, towards yourself and others, you will begin to understand the true meaning of 'Humankind'.

I believe that the ability to forgive and to offer gratitude to ourselves and others is the 'source' or the 'fount' of our emotional intelligence. If you can embrace it, it is a wave you can surf until your dying day.

Sorry is a much bigger word than you might expect

Most people undervalue the power and importance of the word sorry and contrary to popular belief, it is <u>not</u> a hard word to say. Although being truly sorry may be something we have to work at, there are very few scenarios that can't turn out positively, by approaching a negative situation from a place of genuine regret and with a desire to put things right.

Whenever I make a mistake, I always apologise for it, especially when it is something I have done before and someone, like a colleague, friend, or my wife, has called me out on it. Sorry diffuses most scenarios and helps facilitate a way forward.

Even when you do not think that you have done something wrong, but the person you are talking to is upset, it is worth apologising for causing upset, as it was not your intention. This is a productive way of steering the situation towards a positive outcome. If by apologising, you can discuss the situation further with the person concerned, you might find that the thing that caused upset was entirely avoidable and everyone can move forward. By arguing and continuing the upset, you are far less likely to reach a point of reconciliation.

Sorry means nothing without change

Remember, the only way to show that you are truly sorry is by changing your behaviour and making efforts not to do the thing that caused upset again.

This is an important scenario, one that we all need to be more aware of. Both as people who are likely to forgive others for doing things that disadvantaged us or made us feel bad, but also because there is no getting away from the fact that we all make mistakes.

A good friend of mine often says that people who don't make mistakes are not working hard enough. I agree with him! Over the years, I have been repeatedly let down by people who should not have let me down; and yet other people have pleasantly surprised me by not letting me down when I suspected they might. Let me be the first to admit that I have let people down, sometimes knowingly, sometimes totally by accident. Most times, when people have let me down, I will give them another chance…or five! However, if they continue to let me down and make no changes to the way they behave, an apology is unlikely to cut it and I am likely to shut the relationship down.

Talk to someone and make them smile

I do not think that there is a better feeling than making another person smile. Giving someone a compliment about their appearance, whether it's their outfit, hairstyle, or even their fragrance, is a simple way to make someone's day a little brighter and help improve their self-confidence.

(**WARNING**: During the writing of this book I have been informed by my wife, that to say that another person's hair smells nice is weird. Luckily it came up in conversation, after watching a TV program, so I was not put on the weird list, but you may need to be aware of this. So to be clear this is NOT a compliment you should consider. The normal book will now resume).

Here's the thing: the situation must be right and it needs to be done in such a way that you don't appear creepy. I also appreciate that being a northerner, there is often more chat with strangers than there may be in the south. If you are not comfortable giving a compliment to a stranger, you can simply smile as you pass someone or wish someone a good morning or afternoon. I have found that this is easier if you have something in common with a person. Perhaps you are both walking a dog, or you are both walking holding the hand of your partner.

The other thing you can do out of kindness, particularly if you are a bloke, is to try not to make people feel uncomfortable. When we are walking along a quiet street, or behind someone who appears to feel uncomfortable, cross the road, or take a different route, or simply stop and pretend to tie your shoelace to increase the distance between you and the other person. This way, you might help prevent someone from being frightened.

Sometimes advice has to remain advice

I once shared this advice with a colleague and it didn't go quite as expected!

The person in question was in an unhappy marriage; both he and his wife were stubborn people and were were frequent toxic arguments. His wife would make accuse him of things he had done, which he felt were reasonable, but they were not to her liking. He would do things which were not in the spirit of a loving relationship.

One Friday afternoon we were leaving work for the weekend and I shared the following advice with him. I suggested that the next time an incident like this arose he should try to put his pride aside and apologising, irrespective of whether he felt he was in the wrong or not. That way they might be able to have a constructive conversation, and agree a way forward that did not cause further upset. I explained that this could lay the foundations for moving forward and finding a positive outcome which could pave the way towards a healthier relationship.

Monday arrived and I bumped into my colleague. "Mark," he said, "I tried your idea of apologising to my wife."

Cont...

> Cont...
>
> "That's good." I replied, "How did it go?"
>
> He shook his head crossly, exclaiming, "Terribly, actually. There is no changing that woman!!!!"
>
> I asked him to explain precisely what happened?
>
> "Well," he said "I was cleaning the pond out and my wife came in from the shops. She was shouting at me for always making a mess and never cleaning up. She said she wasn't prepared to put up with it anymore. So, I followed your advice and said to her, I'm sorry........ but you're wrong!!!!".
>
> It was at this point I realised that for change to occur, there must also be a desire for it to. Words alone are just wind.
>
> My friend had made it clear on this occasion that there was no such desire for change on either side.

Emotional intelligence

Forgiveness, gratitude and trust are the primary sources of our emotional intelligence. Emotional intelligence or EQ is a person's ability to empathise, appreciate, understand and respond appropriately to another's emotional and metaphorical scenario.

EQ is something that some have in spades. They always know how to respond in the most appropriate way to support others, while other people don't have a clue. They know instinctively when someone wants a hug when sharing difficult information with us or whether they would rather be mauled by a lion!

EQ also helps people read unspoken messages and signs from another person and respond appropriately. The more we know a person, the better chance we have of appropriately responding to their scenario. The better our EQ, the more likely we are to respond appropriately.

Gratitude

It is more important to be grateful and say thank you than to criticise or complain. Always leave feedback for good service and if you have a negative experience and feel that you must leave feedback for that, try to make it constructive and supportive. Consider whether you need to leave it at all. You could just choose to vote with your feet.

We should never compare ourselves with other people. We are all different. Setting goals, ambitions and aspirations based on our observations of what other people have or do is inherently flawed. There will always be someone who has more, a bigger one, or a shinier one. It is a contest that you can never win!

Being grateful for the things you have and for your successes is the truest way to understand satisfaction. If that leads to you establishing what you want and where you would like to be in the future, then so much the better. Do not wish your life away. Do not forget to enjoy the now. You cannot enjoy what has passed or what may come. You can only embrace now, so be careful to cradle it and be present enough to cherish it.

I once heard a saying which has stuck with me for many years, "There is no such thing as good luck, but the harder you work, the luckier you get."

For me, that says it all. Concentrate on the things that you can change and the rest will either happen or it won't. Work hard, look after those you love and be proud of your achievements.

Giving gratitude to those who deserve it

I hated junior school. Too many rules and they treated us like kids! (Imagine that!). But there was one teacher there who got me. Mrs Goodman was new to the school and seemed younger than the other teachers. An excellent teacher, kind and good fun too; she would hand out hundreds of house points for silly things. She liked Star Wars and other TV I was familiar with. We liked the same music too. She also had a picture of Dustin Hoffman on the wall because she fancied him!

In Mrs Goodman's class, I felt respected and understood; she knew we were all humans with the potential to do anything we put our minds to. About ten years ago, I bumped into her. I recognised her because when I was in her class, she told us she had bought her husband a private registration number for his birthday; and I remembered part of the registration number. I also remembered that they had a Volvo.

One day, I was sitting eating lunch in my car, when I noticed a Volvo parked in front of me with a familiar registration number. I thought to myself, "I wonder if…?" and sure enough, Mrs Goodman got out of the car!

She looked the same, although her hair was now silver rather than dark. I got out of my car and approached her, asking if she was who I thought she was. When I explained how I had recognised her, she could not believe it.

I told her who I was and thanked her for everything she had done for younger me, acknowledging I had been a handful and told her she should be very proud for all the good she had done for the world and for all the children who had passed through her care. She seemed very touched by our conversation and I was so happy that I was given an opportunity to thank her face to face.

If ever you get the chance to thank someone who has been a positive influence in your life, grab it with both hands! It is a great pleasure to pass it on and I expect it is a lovely thing to receive.

Another important outside influence was a chap called Kevin Curley (now Kevin Curley MBE). Kevin took groups of teenagers walking in the wilds as part of the Hull and Hessle Hiking Club.

Most of the kids who attended were from my school and he had done this for several years. My brother had been part of the club for six years before me and another friend of mine, Nick Ward, had been in the group on their first outing.

Kevin is a wonderful human. He takes no BS and is highly intelligent. I passionately believe that kids need boundaries and he provided them, taking groups of around ten to fifteen kids all over England, Wales and Scotland. We camped; we stayed in caves; slept in bivy bags outside; and stayed in bothies (old shepherds' huts with very basic facilities in the middle of nowhere). It was amazing. Especially for a wildlife enthusiast like me.

I have stayed in some of the most fantastic locations in the UK, all thanks to Kevin. As kids, we thought we were simply going walking in the wilds with our mates, but looking back, it was so much more than that.

Facebook has brought the members of that group, including Kevin, back together again, both virtually and in person (one positive of social media!) Around twelve years ago, I took my son to meet Kevin near Shap in the Lake District, along with three other former members and we all went to stay at Mosedale Bothy with our families. I expected these modern kids of ours would soon get fed up with Kevin and his assertive ways and rules, but how wrong was I? Within ten minutes, he had them eating out of his hand. I reckon I am good with kids, but this was on another level and magnificent to see as an adult who had known Kevin since being a teenager (See Photo 9 in the photos section).

Being outside and part of nature in such an immersive way is incredibly valuable for mental health and I feel blessed to have this as part of my DNA growing up, thanks to Kevin. I even ran my own successful Bushcraft School, all thanks to the positive influence of Kevin's actions upon the younger me.

> Dear Kevin,
>
> I wish I could inform you of how much good you have brought to my world and, vicariously, that of my friends and family. You are a wonderful, wonderful man. The difference you made to the lives of those young people in the 80's and 90's is not a patch on the life-changing work you do for those under-privileged people living in difficult circumstances in Africa. If one person in the world thinks half as well of me as I do of you when I reach your age, I will think of myself as successful. I can never thank you enough for helping me to understand the need for discipline, endeavour and endurance and the rewards that they may bring.
>
> Thanks!
>
> Mark G

Reconnecting with Kevin, who now does lots of charity work with disadvantaged young people in Sierra Leone, allowed me to thank him properly for the privileges he awarded me with as a teenager.

I cannot think of anything that gives me greater pleasure than being kind. It is its own reward, it is perfection as far as gestures go because everybody wins. Take every opportunity to be kind that you can, it is the ultimate use of energy.

Do good things for others

I have had a beard for over twenty years, ever since I had a jaw operation which left me looking at a different person in the mirror. This knocked my confidence and to this day, I am uncomfortable with my appearance when I do not have a beard.

I am a volunteer for the amazing mental health charity, My Black Dog. In July 2022, I offered to grow my beard without even tidying it up for a whole year and then shave it off to raise money for the charity and improve awareness of mental health.

It was important to me to do something which reflected the purpose of the charity, so making myself vulnerable and challenging my mental health was the decision I made.

That year eventually became eighteen months and in December 2023, Chris Evans invited me onto his Virgin Radio Breakfast Show, where we shaved it off live in the studio.

The volunteers for My Black Dog are not medical professionals, but we have all had our own mental health struggles. This means we all have an idea of what the clients might be going through.

We listen to the clients and share our experience with them to help them make their scenario more manageable. Having someone to talk to in those dark times can make an enormous difference to people, which is the purpose of MBD.

These charities are a crucial support network for people and any donations made are so very vital.

Be kind to others

It is very rewarding to do something kind for somebody at least once a day.

Small gestures are the things that make the world a better place. Letting someone out at a road junction, paying a meal forward, or simply helping someone with something they are stuck with. Being kind is a win-win. It really doesn't matter what your motivation is. Whether you choose to be kind because it makes you feel better; it still helps someone else. Or if you are kind because it helps someone else; it still makes you feel better.

Give thanks for what you have

Think back to what we have said so far about gratitude. The second state of gratitude, which is 'acknowledging the gratitude you have at that moment'. What is it that you are grateful for today?

Maybe you don't have to work with boring Jim from the office because he's on holiday; or perhaps you bought your favourite jam yesterday so you can have it in your sandwiches. You might have been told that you are no longer suffering from the illness you have been experiencing for the past year. Whatever you are grateful for, just write it down. Ideally, list a minimum of three things, but if you have more, go mad and write those down too!

If you are struggling, don't worry. Look at yesterday's answers, or the day before; if they apply, use them. After all, Jim from the office will not be on holiday forever and his feet really honk!

	Three things I'm grateful for today
12.09.24	1. I have food in the cupboard
	2. My Family are healthy and well
	3. Holiday booked for June 2025
13.09.24	1. I remembered to take my lunch to work
	2. Did 10,000 steps
	3. I have a holiday booked for June next year

A blank version of this form is available for your use in Chapter 25.

Look after those who look after you - don't be a Clasper (see glossary for meaning)

When we're finding it hard to manage our emotions, especially during periods of poor mental health, the support of those around us becomes crucial. It's important that we remember that we're the ones behaving out of character, not them. We have a responsibility to show more patience and kindness than we might feel able to. It's not easy, but it really does matter.

Just because you feel off balance, hurt, or unhappy does not give you the right to be cruel or thoughtless to those who are trying to help. You still need to be civil. Why would you help someone who is being a clasper and can be unpredictable towards you? Remember, they are going through this too; they love you and they hurt with you.

Without the help of my amazing wife, the love of my two wonderful lads and close friends, I really do not know what would have happened to me. My wife gave me support through love and through appropriately timed kicks up the arse. Getting back into some kind of work, with routine and responsibility became a vital tool in my recovery. It provided structure, opportunity, distraction and it paid the bills.

I really do wish I had taken those tablets though.

If you are not sure where to turn, there is a section at the end of this book with lots of useful links for organisations who are there to help you. There are also ideas of other places you can go throughout the book. What I would advise as a starter is that you speak to someone you trust, pick someone who will be honest and not necessarily just kind. Sometimes we need the truth to be a little brutal when we are lost. Also don't go asking different people until you get the answer you want to hear, this can be very tempting when you are feeling delicate. If you can't think of friends you can speak to then it's always wise to make an appointment with your GP.

Chapter 19
Meditation, mindfulness and remembering to breathe

What is meditation?

Strictly speaking, I am not sure that what I call meditation is true meditation. What I know is that following these practices has helped me no end. I have also been able to demonstrate my method to others with relative ease and they have found it to be a comfortable approach and useful for quieting the mind.

So here goes…..

When you are first starting out, it is helpful to follow some guided meditation, either by following online videos or audio packages, or by attending classes. I've done both and they each have advantages and disadvantages. I would suggest is that you choose which of these you prefer.

Meditation is an exercise we practise by using our mind rather than our body. The goal is to concentrate all our attention on a single activity, idea, or object to achieve mental clarity, physical and mental calmness, self-awareness and potentially spiritual enlightenment. Meditation in a morning can be a useful way to start your day in a peaceful and positive way and meditation in an evening can help to reduce stress, anxiety and angst accumulated during a busy day. Meditation does not automatically mean relaxation. In fact, when new to it, meditation can be quite frustrating causing the mind to focus on less helpful things. Practice and training help a person hone the skill of meditation.

If you have never tried it, it is hard to appreciate how useful it can be. I also know that it can take several attempts before you appreciate whether it works for you, but please persevere. Don't give up, because if it works for you, it can change your life.

The formal approach on how to meditate

First, it's important to get yourself into a comfortable position. I would suggest that you are sitting upright in an office chair or dining chair, or leaning against something (for people like me with a bad back and an oversized belly).

DO NOT TRY THIS WHILE DRIVING!

I've heard some horror stories about this recently and although they might say you can, it's not a good idea at this stage.

You may find it useful to set a five minute alarm on your watch or your phone. As you get more practiced, you can increase the time until you reach a point that suits you.

It may also help to close your eyes, but I sometimes keep them open. You want to be free from distraction. If you keep your eyes open, let them settle on a point of interest, but not something so engaging it becomes distracting.

Register what you are feeling, cycle through your senses. What can you feel? Consider your points of contact with the ground and the chair. What can you hear? If noise distracts you, you may wish to close a door or window, or even choose a more suitable location. What can you taste? What can you see? If you have your eyes closed, you may see light, or you may not; you may see imagined shapes and colours, etc. Once you have acknowledged these things, you can start your meditation.

Take in a slow deep breath through your nose; if you like, you can count the breaths in and out, or say to yourself 'in' and 'out' in your head. As you do this, you are likely to reach a point where your mind wanders. Once you notice that this has happened, note it, congratulate yourself for noticing it, then return to concentrating on your breathing. The purpose is to keep repeating this and each time you notice your mind wandering, return your attention to your breathing.

Try not to fall asleep. This is the thing I find most difficult. It is also why I devised my alternative approach to meditation.

Using meditation to train my ADHD

Traditional meditation has allowed me to better manage my ADHD.

Just like when I meditate, if I notice that I have been distracted from what I should be doing, I am able to acknowledge the distraction, congratulate myself for noticing it and then return to the task in hand.

This may sound obvious to a person who is not affected by ADHD, but to people like me, life is like walking across a mental minefield. I disappear down rabbit holes of distraction which ultimately lead to a job being half done, or not finished on time. It can be really easy to give yourself a hard time for these distractions. After all, that's what some teachers did at school! Giving yourself a hard time though, is just giving yourself more difficult emotions to manage. By patting yourself on the back and maybe making a note of what you were doing so that you can return to it at some point, you can get on with what you should be doing with limited disruption to your day.

The Pie Eating Man's approach to meditation

If you are struggling to meditate this way because it feels awkward, or a bit "Woo-Woo" there are alternatives. For example, undertake a simple activity like washing up, or digging the garden, or even cleaning the car.

Whatever activity you choose, try to concentrate fully on it. If you find that your mind has strayed to something else, acknowledge that it has happened and return to concentrating on the activity again. That is meditation.

Another good example of this is when you are utterly absorbed in a TV program or when you take a familiar car journey and can't recall any of the places between your starting point and your destination. This is very similar to being in a meditative state.

My preferred form of meditation is 'visualisation meditation'. I favour it because it works for me and when I am using this method, I do not fall asleep. I also find it a pleasant and calming way to meditate, which standard meditation may not always be. In fact, it can be quite distressing and frustrating if you cannot keep a tight rein on your thoughts when your mind drifts.

What is visualisation meditation?

For me, visualisation meditation is a little like having a dream that you are in control of. It can be led by a guide, or you can follow an online video. Once you have done it a few times, you should be able to do it alone without guidance.

You take an activity of your choice and play it out, including all the tiny details. The greater the attention to detail that you pay, the more realistic and helpful you are likely to find the procedure to be. I have used this system many times to examine something I am considering doing thoroughly, such as buying a house, changing my job, or writing a book. It can allow you to recognise and avoid or work around pitfalls and concerns you have about a process before they really happen. The way I mostly use it is to imagine I'm going on holiday in my head.

I start by making myself comfortable, as we have already talked about in the meditation section. Try to sit upright with your feet on the ground, although if I'm honest, the place I do this with the most success is in a swimming pool, or in a hot tub! I'm not sure why that is. I just find being in the water extremely peaceful.

I close my eyes, place my arms in a comfortable position and imagine myself driving to the airport. After parking up in the Meet & Greet car park, I unpack my luggage from the boot, walk to the office and drop off my keys. Then I imagine my wife and me walking into the terminal and queueing up to hand over our cases and show our passports. We have a chat with the person on the counter and go through to Security.

I imagine step by step, going through the airport, security, buying aftershave in the duty free and getting on the plane. There are no limits. You can choose to turn left into business class on the plane. Imagine the drinks you'll order and the food you will eat, etc. (this is probably the closest I will ever get to business class).

The plane arrives and we collect our luggage and get in a taxi to our hotel; I imagine the hotel reception and our room; we go to bed and wake up to the wonder of tropical sunshine. We get up, go for breakfast, I imagine what we eat, decide whether to set up by the pool or on the beach. There we make our plans for the next day; do we sit by the pool? Take part in activities? Go diving or visiting local places of interest?

I imagine what I might drink around the pool, decide whether to have an alcoholic drink or something else. I imagine whether there will be music (normally reggae, in my head) and if so, what sort?

I imagine the heat at the height of the day, taking a dip in the pool, going snorkeling and as the day goes on I wonder whether I might sit at the bar and watch the sun go down, if we will take an early dinner and what we will wear. I try to imagine the birds, the insects, the lizards, the stickiness of a spilt drink on the floor, the smell and the feel of the towels on the sunbed.

This approach to meditation has brought me amazing clarity, allowing me to explore the pros and cons of future plans to such an extent that it has helped me make better financial decisions for my family. We have even taken trips we might not have otherwise and it's been a real boost for my mental well-being.

It has meant that I have also been able to appreciate more traditional forms of meditation and take part in those. It was the first thing I really got into, which made me think about writing this book. There is an element of society who has traditionally written off these methods as daft, pointless, or a waste of time. I was one of those people and I was wrong.

Another reason I like it is that it distracts the mind, but with 'something', as opposed to 'nothing'. When your mind is already overflowing with noise caused by the mental health scenario you find yourself in, even sitting in the quiet can be overwhelming. By adding a narrative, you distract the mind rather than place it in the quiet. We are all busy people although, once you get a hang of traditional mediation, it is possible to transition between that and life. In the early stages, it is easier to transition from a noisy, busy life to an activity rather than a concept. Other things I like to think about when using this method include:

- I scuba dive, getting on the boat, setting up my gear, imagining the dive and the creatures I encounter
- Building my dream house, I locate, design, plan and oversee the building of the house and gardens
- I design rooms (similar to the above)
- Setting up camp in the woods, I walk into the woodlands, find a pleasant location, clean the camp, build a shelter, get a fire going, cook a meal and so on
- I drive journeys in my head that I know well

This list is not exhaustive and can include anything that you like to do.

Newcomers to meditation often believe they will require a peaceful and quiet environment. It appears most people who practice meditation would agree, but the proper answer would be that you can do it anywhere you feel comfortable and at peace. If you want to listen to whale song, do it! If you want to listen to ACDC, do that!

I recently went for a walk in the woods with my wife where we heard a cuckoo. We stopped to listen to it and although our focus was on that sound, I found the sounds of all the other bird songs amazing and very peaceful. So, I made a five minute recording of it on my phone and now I can loop that whenever I want to meditate, listening to it repeatedly. You can do that with a V8 engine if that's what flicks your switch.

Mindfulness

I am not really a sporty person, but I did used to run places as a kid and I did a lot of swimming. My preferred stroke when I was young was back stroke. This means that for most of the time, the ears are underwater and the eyes are looking up at the ceiling. When swimming like this, all you can hear is your heartbeat and your breath. I tuned into the rhythm of it and became all consumed in what I was doing. I didn't know it at the time, but I was in the moment; I was present. When I think about how many hours I spent in the pool as a kid, it's amazing I'm not a monk. It is what people describe as getting 'in the zone'; when you are taking part in an activity while unaware of the surrounding environment. I would almost forget where I was, listening to the beat of my heart and the rhythm of my breathing in my head.

Mindfulness is a practice that helps people tame their thoughts and feelings. It combines an awareness of ourselves and the environment around us and encourages us to pay attention to the present moment without judgement. Many mental health practices encourage the use of mindfulness techniques alongside their specific purpose.

At this point, I just want to pause. As mentioned in the 'Woo Woo Warning' at the beginning of the book, I know topics like this can put people off. But to truly understand something and decide if it's worth anything to us, we need to give it a fair shot. That doesn't mean diving in headfirst we just need to be open minded enough to think about it, explore it a little and see if it is something that might work for us. Writing it off simply because our mates don't do it, or because we've decided "people like us" don't do stuff like this, is… well, daft.

You don't need to do any of this in public. Nobody has to know you're even thinking about it. We all carry a smartphone or have access to a laptop — everything you need is quite literally at your fingertips.

So, give these things a go. If they don't click the first time, try again. And if, in the end, it's still not for you, what have you lost? There's nothing to be ashamed of and nothing to feel embarrassed about. But it just might have a significant, positive impact on your life.

Mindful breathing and breathwork

Scuba diving - breathing like my life depends on it

My absolute favourite thing to do in the entire world is Scuba Diving. Even better if I can be with my wife, son and friends who also take part in the sport. As the title of this book suggests, I'm a big lad. I'm overweight and although I am relatively fit, I could do with being much fitter. If you don't scuba dive, you probably don't know that the length of time you can stay underwater is determined by the air you have available.

Although everyone starts with the same amount of air, divers go through their air more quickly if they are carrying more weight.

In fact, divers are at a higher risk of encountering difficulties if they are larger, dive to greater depths, are dehydrated, experience anxiety or overexertion, have consumed too much alcohol, or breathe rapidly or uncontrollably.

In almost all scenarios, divers perform dives in groups of two or more for safety reasons. There is a rule that once one person in the group reaches half a tank, the group turns back towards the start, which means they should be back at the start with a safety cushion of air left so that they can safely ascend. The only issue with this is that if you are the biggest and the lumpiest of the group, you are likely to be the person who ends the dive first each time. Although there is rarely blame attached to this, it doesn't feel nice to be 'that person'.

Most diving instructors and guides are very fit and can manage their use of air incredibly well. My wife is petite and…well, she could be taller! She regularly comes up with more air left than the dive guides. Being the larger, lumpier one, I feel pressured not to be the person in the group to call short the dives for others. After all, we have all paid to be there.

Given the physical obstacles I face, I have had to learn to put significant concentration into my breathing and my breath management. I must breathe calmly and slowly, avoid any sort of panic and pause at both the top and the bottom of my breaths easier said than done with a number of seven foot sharks circling you). Again, to do this safely, I must remain very aware of my buoyancy underwater. Holding your breath as a diver is an absolute no-no. If you hold in a breath for any length of time, you will float to the surface and find yourself in a world of pain. This can be deadly. If you do not have enough air in your lungs, you can sink and panic, or even worse, drown.

Avoiding this takes a conscious, careful balance of slow breaths in, pausing, slow breaths out and pausing. Breathing in this way can lengthen a dive to an hour or more, as opposed to thirty five to forty five minutes when breathing recklessly.

I feel more at peace when I am diving than anywhere else. Particularly when I am lucky enough to be diving in tropical seas with breathtaking marine life. Every dive I take part in might be my last for so many reasons, so I eke out every second of being down there. (See Photo 10 in the photos section)

When combined with intentional and mindful breathing, I feel as though I am looking through a window into what heaven will look like if it exists.

Until I sat down to write this book, I had never made the link between breathing and meditation and the meditative state I find myself in when I dive.

Have you ever heard the saying, "Imitation is the sincerest form of flattery"? Well, something diving has taught me is that not only is there some truth in that, but imitation has actually made me a better diver. You see kids doing it all the time on the football pitch, copying that amazing free kick they saw the night before. (I can still remember doing just that with my mates the day after Roberto Carlos scored that screamer against France in '97.)

I'd waited twenty nine years to finally get the chance to learn to dive and I was determined to take it seriously. So, I copied the dive guide. I moved slowly, kept my hands in and used my fins instead of flailing my arms about. And because of that, I got pretty good and quickly. Before long, people assumed I'd been diving for years. What I realised was that the instructors moved that way for a reason: it made them more efficient at moving and breathing underwater. It also helped them get closer to wildlife without disturbing it which, for me, was the whole point of being down there.

Since then, I've tried the same approach with other skills I've picked up and it works, give it a go! I reckon the reason we're often put off from copying others like this is because it can make us feel a bit daft, or we worry that others will think we're just being sycophantic. But really, it's just another example of kids being little geniuses. As adults, we sometimes let vanity get in the way of learning and doing well.

Breathwork

Breathwork is when we take part in intentionally controlled breathing exercises with a view to positively affecting our overall wellness. Breath work is often used to 'centre' us in the 'now' or the 'present' as part of yoga, meditation and even exercise.

There are lots of audiobooks, podcasts and online videos about breathwork, which often go hand in hand with yoga and/or meditation. These are helpful, particularly if you are just learning about breathing techniques.

There are two main types of breathwork: 'mindful breathing' and 'deep breathing'. My knowledge of breathwork is limited, but I find it very interesting. I was quite skeptical but had a surprisingly enlightening experience which changed my mind. I have tried both mindful breathing and deep breathing exercises. The latter provided me with such a natural high, it amazed me.

All mindful breathing requires is your lungs and some time and possibly your phone or TV for guidance if you are new to it. So, it is available to anyone. Breathwork can improve our happiness levels, clarity of thought and reduce stress.

Mindful breathing is very similar and usually incorporates breathing exercises.

Bringing mindfulness and mindful breathing practices together, we help to better understand how it feels to be in the present, helping us to live in the moment.

It makes sense that specific breathing techniques can be beneficial. After all, breathing is essential for our organs to function properly. We inhale oxygen, which oxygenates our blood, purifying and regulating our life force. Then, we exhale the used air, which contains a higher concentration of carbon dioxide. Most of us under use our lungs and need to take part in breathing exercises to make the most of the benefits that they can provide us with (other than the obvious ones).

Nature has all you need, just open your senses

When you are out and about, inhale the smells, hear the sounds, feel the wind, splash in puddles, watch the clouds, notice the different colours and textures of trees. I used to have a bushcraft business. I would take families into the woods and teach them how to light fires, how to build shelters using forest floor materials, knife skills and cooking over an open fire. It was a wonderful way to get people into the outdoors, especially young people and show them the wonder of nature.

I used to ask the children how they would draw a tree. They would describe drawing a brown trunk and green leaves. Then I would ask them to show me one tree, out of the many that were around us, which looked like the trees they described. "Find me one tree with a brown trunk," I would say.

Obviously, they couldn't. Tree trunks, branches and leaves have many colours and textures. I would tell them to find as many different types of tree trunks as they could and to touch them and feel the differences between them. I taught them that those differences showed different varieties of trees; some were green, some were red and some were silver. They always took great interest in this and became fascinated by the insects they saw when looking more closely at the trunks and the veins of the leaves. Noticing the world all around us more closely is a wonderful path to being present and mindful in nature.

Other therapeutic activities

Relaxation

A visit to a health spa, with access to saunas and Jacuzzis, can be a very pleasurable way to reduce anxiety. Book a treatment, such as a massage and enjoy being pampered.

Yoga

Yoga is a relaxing form of exercise in which people adopt specific physical positions designed to both stretch and exercise muscles in the body. With links to spirituality and mindfulness to help exercise and relax the mind at the same time. There is plenty of evidence that Yoga helps people to manage and reduce anxiety levels.

Massage

As mentioned above having a massage relaxes the muscles in the body and helps to reduce the amount of cortisol produced by the body. This increases overall relaxation levels, lowers the heart rate and helps to release hormones such as serotonin, which naturally lifts an individual's mood.

Chapter 20

Goals, bucket lists & plans

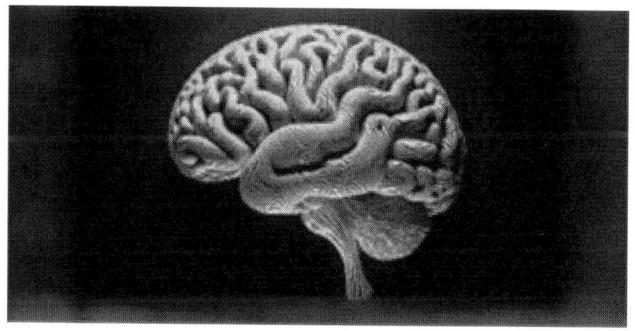

Make short and long term plans

You can't achieve your dreams if you don't know what they are. The best way to do this is to write them down.

Write a bucket list or five

Most people who have a bucket list don't have more than one and they rarely write them down. They are just things that they are very passionate about that rattle around in their heads with a vague desire to carry them out one day. This is where we change that. We are going to write them down, so we don't forget about them.

I have come up with five types of bucket list to consider. Viewed together, they should help to maximise their value. Yes, I know this sounds like a pain in the bum, but bear with me.

When I explain what I mean, I think you will understand and find it useful and maybe even fun.

My five categories of bucket list are:

1. Short Term achievable in a year
2. Life-time bucket list
3. Remembering bucket list items you have achieved
4. Revisiting old lists
5. Local attraction bucket lists

Short term achievable in a year

This one is a little like a New Year's list of things you would like to achieve. I don't suppose it is essential for all these things to be achieved in one year, but this list should comprise things that are within reach.

Things that are within your financial constraints, examples include - learning to knit, visiting a premier league football game or attending a music festival. They should still be special to you, but they don't need to be earth shatteringly expensive. They are likely to need some sort of investment of time, money or dedication to complete.

Life-time bucket list

When I was about three years old, my mum's partner and his son sailed from Whitby to Australia on a converted trawler and I can clearly remember hearing tales of things they saw and experienced during this epic journey.

My exposure to this adventure influenced my interest in many things and planted seeds in my mind of things that I would love to see as I grew older.

Many children have an imaginary friend, well I had an imaginary trip to Australia. I would sit with my mum watching programs like David Attenborough's wildlife programs and Alan Whicker's travel programs, which were filmed in wild and wonderful locations. When watching them, I'd say to my mum, I saw one of those when I went to Australia, or I ate that on my trip to Australia.

I believe these fantasies mixed with the photos and stories I heard helped forge many of my lifelong ambitions, such as my wish to see a coconut palm tree, go scuba diving with sharks and see iguanas on a rocky Caribbean shore.

These were my first lifelong ambitions.

Life time Bucket List
Visit Australia
Live abroad – somewhere hot with great diving
Learn to drive a Truck
See a Hammerhead Shark, a Whale Shark & a Manta ray
Fly somewhere First Class

A blank version of this form is available for your use in Chapter 25.

Remembering bucket list items you have achieved

Just because you have ticked off certain aims on your bucket lists does not mean that you can't look back on them and enjoy them again. Consider creating a scrapbook or memory box using ticket stubs, photos and other memorabilia. You could even write yourself a letter almost like a diary entry saying what you enjoyed, who you were with and what surprises you encountered.

If you don't write them down, it's easy to forget how important they were to you. You can even forget them altogether, which would be a great shame.

Bucket List Items achieved
See Billy Connolly Live
Visit Egypt
Learn to speak basic Arabic
Become a qualified SCUBA diver
Visit and Dive in the Red Sea with my family
Buy a house
Write a book
Dive with Sharks
See a coconut palm tree in the wild
See bioluminescence in the sea
See Paul Heaton play live
See Bill Bailey live

A blank version of this form is available for your use in Chapter 25.

Revisiting the list

By keeping old bucket lists which show the ones you have ticked off, you can remember the places you went and things you did. Those places and activities may have changed since you visited. Perhaps your circumstances have changed and you could now take part in things you wanted to but, in the past, could not afford. The political circumstances of a location could have changed since you visited and there are more freedoms available to see parts you could not visit before. Whatever the reason, revisiting items on your bucket list can be great fun and a pleasant way to revisit the nostalgia of your past.

Bucket list items to revisit

Bucket List item	Revisit and why
Qualify as a SCUBA diver	Qualify as an advances SCUBA diver to be able to visit special underwater locations
Visit Egypt	SCUBA in famous Red Sea Dive locations
Seeing a coconut palm tree in the wild	Drink from a coconut straight from the tree

A blank version of this form is available for your use in Chapter 25.

Local attraction bucket list

This is a bucket list we should all consider writing, but most people overlook. The idea is to write a list of landmarks and experiences local to you that tourists travel to enjoy, with a view to you visiting them yourself. It is so easy to overlook them because you live near to them and they become part of the background of a location. Most big towns and cities have things like this and the bigger the place, the more likely there are to be some.

An excellent example of this is that we live by the sea and we have lived by the sea for over twenty-five years. We love nature and marine wildlife and every year there are reports of dolphins and whales to be seen on an almost daily basis in the summer from the foreshore (which is an 800m walk from our front door). You even can take boat rides from the harbour to see them!

Each time we see posts about them on social media, my wife and I look at each other and curse, saying, "Why don't we ever see them?" The reason we don't see them is that we do not put any effort in; to look for them, or to go on the boat trips when there are reports saying they are in the area. So next year that is what we are going to do.

General rules for all five bucket lists

You should update your bucket lists whenever you think of things you have done or would like to do. Why not keep them on your mobile phone? Most of us have our phone with us all the time.

You could even keep a diary and log each event achieved. When I dive, I keep a dive log of all that I have seen and done on each individual dive. I include the location, the people I was with, even what equipment I used. When I go back and read through my dive logs, it's incredible how quickly I am taken back to those dives. It also reminds me of the places I want to go back to, given the chance.

Have things in your diary to look forward to

Taking a holiday is very important. Having a break from the serious stuff and enjoying wholesome time alone or with loved ones and friends helps us to recharge our batteries and to remind us to know them better and love them more deeply.

No matter what holiday you choose, they can be expensive. This is the obstacle that many people struggle to overcome. I understand this. When times were hard, either we didn't get to have a holiday, or we booked a cheap camping break. As I have mentioned, I love to travel abroad, but I am terrible at making a decision when there are so many options out there. I also have a terrible fear of spending the family holiday fund on a holiday which we do not enjoy.

So, the whole process of booking a holiday can be a problem for me. Being a diver has meant that I have been able to combine my hobby with my holiday destinations, which really helps to reduce the option of locations available to me. We invariably end up holidaying in Egypt because of this. We find the holidays there to be affordable and we love the sun. Because we have been there a few times, we have been able to pick up some of the language and can have a basic conversation in Arabic.

Taking the time to learn some of the language before and during our holidays has enhanced our enjoyment of them tenfold. Understanding some of what people say and being able to share jokes with local people in their language breaks down barriers between cultures and has opened doors and made us feel more welcome than normal (which we didn't think possible).

We have made lifelong friends with other holidaymakers, as well as staff and people that live in Egypt who we remain in regular contact with.

Enjoy the build up

I get such a lot of joy and contentment from anticipating forthcoming occasions. Events like holidays abroad, diving excursions, breaks from work with my wife and meeting up with friends. I have been known to print off a countdown calendar up to six months before my holidays and mark off each day as they passed.

I am able to use this anticipation of events I know I will love, to assist me through days that I do not enjoy, or that I find hard. My wife and I both use it to 'gee' each other on, when we think that is needed.

The actual events tend to be so short lived and they can feel as though they are over in a heartbeat, but for me the anticipation period before means that time periods of the events feel as though they are extended. It gives me time to plan the things I want to do, the clothes I will need or if I need to take any equipment with me. It helps to give me time to research the location and the best places to visit. If I'm travelling abroad, I usually take the time to learn some of the language which always comes in handy.

Living this way allows me to take joy from an event before it has even happened.

Chapter 21
Toolkit for a healthy mind

My strengths and weaknesses

One of my biggest flaws growing up was that I interrupted people while they were speaking. I did it because my mind raced ahead, thinking up questions or thoughts so quickly that if I didn't get them out straight away, they'd vanish like smoke. If I waited for my turn to speak, I'd often forget what I was going to say.

Even writing things down didn't always help, I'd forget what the notes meant after a short while. This, combined with another of my less endearing habits (anticipating what people are going to say before they've said it), meant I'd jump in too early. I'd interrupt not just because I thought I already knew what they were about to say, but also because I was panicking that I'd forget my own point.

I've since realised that I don't, in fact, know what someone is going to say and there's real value in listening properly, all the way through. The bits I used to miss by interrupting were often the most important.

It's also just a really annoying habit. So, over the past six years, I've made a real effort to stop. I'm pleased to say I've improved a lot. I now understand how valuable proper listening is, not just for hearing things accurately, but for building trust and strengthening relationships with the people I'm talking to.

My Pro's & Con's	
Pro's	Con's
I give a good cuddle	I can be (very) annoying
I do what I say I will	I spread myself too thinly
I'm always on time	I underestimate my abilities
I am very fair	I can be annoyingly fair
I'm very brave	My bravery can make me reckless
I can & will keep a secret	I'm not good at accepting compliments

A blank version of this form is available for your use in Chapter 25.

Once you have analysed your pros and cons, reflect on them are there things that you want to change

The next thing to do is imagine yourself as someone else, a friend looking in and reading what has been written.

Now imagine that they have asked you what you feel about the things they have listed about them.

1. Is that something that you think they should change?
2. Is it something that you can think of a way of changing?
   If yes, make a note of that.
3. If they change, are they likely to feel better?

What makes you tick?
What motivates you?

This sounds easy, but have you ever sat down and thought about the things that make you the person you are? The person you would like to be? And the things in your heart which you are passionate about or feel strongly about? The core values that drive you and the things on which you are unshakable? (See Chapter sections on fixed self and fluid self).

Write them down and actively take the time to consider them.

First, see what they do for you, explore why you believe in them and decide if you would like to change any of them. If so, why? And if you have a why, then it should be your aim to find a how, which you can do alone or with others. I try to do this as regularly as I can. Just as your palette changes as you get older, so can your core beliefs.

What makes you happy?

To aim for happiness, you need to identify the things that make you happy. I appreciate there are many answers to this question, depending on the context and the scenario. In the end, though, is that such a bad thing?

Would it be terrible to keep a list of everything you think of that makes you happy? From watching an ant go about their business; from a sun lounger on holiday; to driving in the Paris to Dakar Rally, write a list. You can also keep a record of when you do the things that make you happy.

You may see that things that make you level ten happy are not happening very often, because you are busy doing things that only make you level four happy. Once you know this, you can investigate ways of shifting that balance to suit you better.

Look at these questions below and write down your answers:

What makes you happy?

How happy does that make you?

How often are you doing any of them?

If you are not, why not?

If you are not, how could you start?

And so on.

What made you tick as a kid?

Some activities, music and passions I enjoyed as a kid, can be rewarding and comforting to go back to and have a go at. For some people, it be colouring-in, for others it might be certain music, or even a kick around in the park. Thinking about the things I liked to do as a kid provides me with an activity I enjoyed when I had a level of unshakable stability in my life and fewer concerns.

I love singing.

I love music.

I love audiobooks - some may consider this a dumbed down way to read books, but WHO CARES? If it works for you, do it! I have "read" dozens of books I never would have if I hadn't used audio books. I have also listened to many books that I enjoyed in my youth.

Explain the value of this and grounding yourself, you might think it feels daft, you might have the freedom, but just have it as a floating piece of wood in in the sea when there is nothing else, it is something to hold onto and perhaps start to build a floating island from.

Mental health and medication

I am not a doctor. I cannot advise or comment on specific approaches to medication. However, what I would say is that medication prescribed by your GP can be a pivotal step in managing mental health conditions. Remember that it may take a little while to find the right path for you and if the first medication does not work, or has side effects, please go back and ask for more help and be open to trying alternative medications or solutions.

Don't self-medicate with drugs and/or alcohol

When dealing with any mental health issue, unless otherwise advised by a medical expert, it is wise to avoid alcohol, drugs and other artificial stimulants. These are often a temporary solution and their use causes more problems than they help.

Unfortunately, all too often, mental illness can be the reason that people turn to drugs and alcohol. Many people describe it as a way to self-medicate their problems.

People say that it 'quietens their mind', or 'numbs the pain', or it may just be that it seems to help them sleep. Ironically, many types of drugs, alcohol and other artificial stimulants can make it more likely that a person will suffer from a mental health illness. They can muddy the water, making it more difficult to treat these conditions. Equally, the effects that are beneficial in the early stages of use casually dissipate with regular use.

Most people find that the self-medication initially lifts their mood, but the comedown takes them lower than they were before the self-medicated high. This cycle continues until the high reached is nowhere near what was originally the normal that people are trying to escape. It's the perfect example of a downward spiral which is very difficult to stop once started. Alcohol may help a person to relax and fall asleep initially, but it usually causes poor patterns of sleep resulting in the individual feeling worse rather than better.

Medical professionals often refer to someone with a mental health issue, who also uses drugs as a dual diagnosis. If you do not already receive support from a local mental health service, make an appointment with a GP. They should decide what the most appropriate next step is, such as medication, therapy, or a combination of the two. They may also refer you to a drug and alcohol service to assist with dealing with that side of the diagnosis.

Chapter 22
Getting to know You & helping yourself

You owe it to yourself

If I have learned one thing during my life it is that although other people may help and assistance may be available to me. The only person who owes me anything is me and the only person I can on hundred percent rely upon to do what I ask is me.

I have an amazing wife and supportive friends and family and I am confident that if I needed help, it would be made available to me, but I cannot expect that.

I also cannot expect someone else to pick up the slack created by me.

So, when times are hard and I am suffering, I know that I MUST be the person to make the first move to my own improvement. If I don't why should someone else?

That said, if I am aware of someone in that situation, I would like to think that I would help them even if they didn't seem to have it in them to help themselves. Sometimes camaraderie and care from another person is the catalyst for a person to be able to kickstart their road to recovery.

Loyalty web

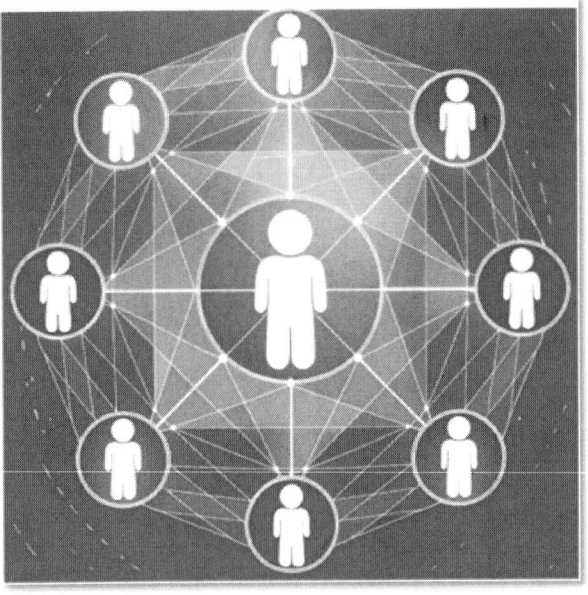

Loyalty web diagram

I created this diagram some years ago as part of a leadership course I was on. I called it the Loyalty Web and it shows the value of a collective who chooses to offer one another care, trust, honesty and kindness. Our friends, family, colleagues and loved ones can all be a part of the Loyalty Web.

Imagine each person in your support network holds a fine strand which connects you to them and that is the same for all the people in their networks and so on and so forth.

Everyone in your network will have strands connecting to many people and the support networks of each of those people will have strands connecting to more people, creating a complex web of overlapping connections.

The diagram shows a group of individuals sharing "positivity strands," creating a web. The more people that are involved in the web, the stronger the web becomes. If an individual has a difficult period and they need to let go for a time, then they can rest on the web. Eventually, when they are feeling strong enough, they can hold their strands again.

The more people that belong to the loyalty web, the more capable it is of supporting people who are struggling. It is strongest when people participate in an authentic way, sharing their situation and if needed, allowing their support network to step in and avoid people falling into crisis.

If you think about it, most employers should strive to propagate these behaviours, to keep people well. The web then becomes self-sustaining as far as wellbeing goes.

The web can be weakened or destroyed altogether if people fail to be authentic and true or if they are dishonest or uncaring. It is also important that people do not spend too long resting on the web, taking advantage of those holding it together. When this happens, people will cut the strands and the support for those taking more than their fair share will fall away.

The Loyalty web can stand losing people, provided that the remaining people continue to stand strong for each other. However, if there are not enough people supporting the web, or too many people are taking advantage, participants may turn away from the web and divert their energy into the strands of other webs they are connected with.

When all participants play their part, the Loyalty Web can form an extremely strong emotional, professional and motivational system.

Many people do not feel as though they are part of an existing loyalty web. If this is the case we have a responsibility as individuals to seek out opportunities to take part in such a group. By joining hobby groups, sports teams, adult learning classes, local coffee mornings and lunch meetings, you can find like-minded people who you are able to grow bonds with.

It is also very important that, if we are a part of such a group, we make an effort to look out for people who we feel may benefit from being a part of it too. Often people who need these links the most are the people who feel least comfortable in actively seeking them out.

Faith and spiritualism

I love singing happy songs on a sunny morning when I am driving to work. Although I am not a religious person, I loved singing the songs and hymns in assembly at school, songs like 'Morning has Broken' and 'When a knight won his spurs'.

I remember driving into work one morning; the sun was out and my windows were down. My forty minute commute is along the coastline of the stunning Yorkshire Wolds. Although I don't believe that an all-powerful God created the wonderful scene I was enjoying, the wonder of nature takes my breath away. I don't know what the source of creation is or what the Big Bang (as we scientists refer to it) was. But what I do know is that it's amazing and if I could write songs about it, I would! If they could capture the beauty of nature as 'Morning has broken' does, then I would be a happy person.

Walking into work that morning, I remember speaking with my friend and colleague who found God in his mid-forties and I told him how envious I was of him because I knew the comfort that he found in his unfailing faith in the existence of God.

I have had the same conversation with another friend. They pray each day for those they love and give thanks for the good things they have in their life and they find comfort in prayer, although they hold no specific religious beliefs. Perhaps this means they are spiritual.

Show me someone who's never said 'thank you' to no one in particular when something went their way, or never quietly asked for help when things got tough, even if they don't believe in a higher power. They may not be religious, but in those moments, they're still reaching out to something beyond themselves. That, in itself, feels like a kind of faith.

I like my friend's approach and I probably do something similar, just not as part of a daily ritual. It works for him, though and it might work for you.

Change is our responsibility

What brings me joy and what does not? The table below shows my Joy and Worry list. It includes a list of things which bring me comfort, joy and relaxation and things which cause me anxiety, worry and distress.

Writing these things down makes them real and more recognisable to me. This helps me to recognise the scenarios I want to aim towards and those that may put me at risk and I should avoid.

It can also help me see if there are any patterns that exist between them, so that I can see whole areas of activities and behaviour that I might want to encourage or avoid. I may also want to look at some things I wish to work on and change because they are traits I am uncomfortable with.

My Joy & Worry lists	
What brings me joy & Relaxation?	What brings me anxiety Worry & Distress?
Being around inspiring people	Unintentionally causing upset
Being surrounded by nature	Interrupting people as they speak
Singing	Unfair treatment
Scuba Diving	Mixed messages relating to important matters

A blank version of this form is available for your use in Chapter 25.

My hobbies

Hobbies and interests are incredibly valuable. Until you have some, you might not realise just how important they are.

Depending on the hobby, we can find all kinds of positive stimulation which can aid our physical and mental health. They are an excellent way of meeting people, particularly those with whom we have a shared interest. This is of tremendous benefit to us and good example of the Loyalty Web at work.

I am not a natural sports person. I'm just not competitive and I never really have been. Most of my childhood friends were mainly into football. I think if any of them had had mental health issues, they would have seen support in that world. As I have already mentioned, I swam a lot as a kid, but I reduced that significantly when I was about eleven. Because of this, I didn't really have hobbies in my teenage years. By the time I went to Uni, drinking beer was probably my favourite hobby and to be fair, I got pretty good at that!

In recent years, as my finances have improved and I have got to know myself a bit better, I have pursued some hobbies, things I've always wanted to have a go at but didn't think I had the finances or the time.

Note: I have many different hobbies over the years. As far as I can tell from speaking to other people with the condition this seems to be a trait of ADHD. It would seem that we undertake a hobby, (often obsessively, this is definitely the case for me) until we reach a level at which we feel as though we are able to complete the task to a high enough standard, then we move on to the next 'shiny activity'.

You really do have time! - You just need to allocate it

Growing up, I was not exposed to skills like DIY and woodwork, so I was not very practical or adept at these things. This was another example of toxic masculinity affecting my life as an adult. There is an expectation that men know this stuff. All the other men in my daily life; my grandad, my uncle and my friend's dads were all good at it.

Because of this, I have tried many courses and hobbies to compensate for what I felt was a weakness or deficiency in my life. Here's the list of some of the 'compensatory' hobbies I've had a go at:

Dry stone walling - which was wonderful. It was like being in an episode of The Darling Buds of May, an instant depression suppressor. Although I imagine it would be a lot less fun on a January day in the pouring rain,

Green Woodwork - Building my own draw horse and pole lathe and learning to use both. They are wonderful crafts and very good for the soul. I also did an axe sharpening course, which was very useful for keeping all my tools, axes, chisels and knives sharp. Most people don't realise that blunt tools are much more dangerous than razor sharp ones.

Blacksmithing – I really enjoy blacksmithing, it's one of those things that most people never get a chance to try. After a few years of tinkering, I now have a forge and anvil of my own. I'm a steward on the ironwork and blacksmithing stand at the Great Yorkshire Show where I help alongside some truly fabulous blacksmiths, (I'm just a hobbyist) although I have won a few amateur prizes. There really is no comparison to taking a piece of cold hard steel, getting it hot and shaping it as if it were plasticine. It's a real rush.

Bushcraft - I ended up running my own beginner's bushcraft business for nearly ten years, teaching adults and children how to build shelters, light fires and introducing them to basic blacksmithing. I love wildlife and have a good knowledge of nature and plants and it was a joy to share that knowledge.

Along with the theme of DIY and compensatory knowledge, there is another pattern to all of the above. They are all ancient crafts which are basic in nature but require a skilled hand to carry out to a high level. Although this link was not a conscious one, I think my love of nature, my observations of the outdoors and the countryside and my curiosity of a simpler life, must have been the unconscious driver for these interests.

I now have such wonderful friends as a result of taking part in these hobbies, people I would have no hesitation in inviting to my home and sharing my concerns with. I am very lucky.

I also have other hobbies which are very important to me and my mental health. I go through phases of which hobby I take part in, this is also likely to be due to my ADHD and the need to switch between different interests to satisfy my chaotic mind.

Board gaming - I attend what we call 'nerd club' every week with other people who enjoy playing board games in person. Again, I have made good friends doing this and it is not uncommon for us to have conversations about each other's mental health. We have found that we all have matters that benefit from safe discussion from time to time. We do this at a local café, where the wonderful Karyn takes good care of us, making lovely food for us. She makes the best tiffin in the land!

Cookery - I enjoy cookery. I particularly like making Chinese food and homemade pizza. It's a great way to be mindful. I like to whack on some music, or an audio book, or a footy game on the radio and just throw my mind into creating tasty food. Don't let cooking intimidate you. Everyone can cook a tasty meal and the more you do it, the more you get a knack for it.

Scuba diving - I have a lifelong interest in wildlife, particularly marine life. I have always felt drawn to water; I'm intrigued by watching the way in which life behaves under water. Over the past eleven years, I have visited Egypt several times with my family. During that time, my Grandma North sadly passed away and left me a little money. I used that money to get my wife, my son and me qualified as PADI open water divers. Since then, we have all qualified as PADI Advanced open water divers and we have had the privilege of gathering over one hundred dives each in various places across the world. To say that this had been my greatest ambition until this point in my life would be an understatement and I hope it is something my grandma would have approved of me doing.

Hobbies in general - More often than not, I believe that hobbies allow us to be distracted from our everyday scenario and encourage us to concentrate on them. They are usually something that require our concentration in order for us to continue to improve our ability to do whatever the task is. Without realising it we are required to be present, mindful and in the moment.

During a game of football for example in order to win the team needs to be aware of what is going on the pitch, who has the ball, who will be there to win it back, how can the team work together in the most effective way to score and ultimately win the game.

When making a good joint between two pieces of wood,

you need to consider the pressures that will be upon that joint when it is in use and at what angles those pressures will occur. This will help to inform which the most appropriate jointing technique should be used and what tools are required to do that. You have to measure carefully and be precise when making the cuts. All of this requires planning, understanding and concentration, which is very difficult if we are not present, mindful and in the moment, the quality of the work we carry out is likely to be lessened by distractions.

Helping out and volunteering

I really enjoy helping people out, whether that be at my children's sports clubs, the charity work I do at My Black Dog or helping at outdoor events. According to those around me, I can sometimes be too eager to help people and I need to ensure that I am not taken advantage of. That said, I usually only allow that to happen once. I enjoy helping people so much that I am happy to write these events off as collateral damage. Most people are good and very few people ask for help when they need it.

My theory on a sixth sense

I have already mentioned the visit I had to the Middle East as a kid. When I was there, I noticed something which has influenced a theory I have. That theory is that we humans have a sixth sense.

As with many places in the Middle East, the locations we visited had powerful connections with religion, religious beliefs and history. My family and I are not religious and we did not visit these places for this reason, but it was everywhere and could not be avoided.

There was a special feeling in some of these places that

we all felt and it was more than the fact that they were of interest and historical significance. In my life, I have only ever felt similar feelings or emotions when I have been at large music festivals, big football games, or large gatherings, such as Hull Fair, or the Blackpool illuminations.

It is this that has led me to believe that we humans give off some kind of energy that other humans can feel when we gather in groups and pour out our emotions. I think that we are sensitive to this energy. I think it is why humans like to gather in pubs and listen to music, or why we like to attend firework displays, or New Year's Eve celebrations in large cities. It may also be why some people don't like these events. In my experience, the emotions and energy they create can be strong and can cause tears, which some people may find overwhelming or uncomfortable.

Chapter 23
How can I help someone else?

If you are anything like me and have struggled with your mental health, you might like to consider helping someone else who looks like they are heading towards a similar scenario. I hope this book will also be useful to those looking to support a friend or loved one.

With that in mind, I am confident that most of the issues I have discussed in the book should be of use, but it would be remiss of me not to include a section specifically on how to help others. What I have learned over the years is that nobody is the same. Everybody has their own preferences regarding the help and support they require.

Are you really ready?

The first and most important thing to note is that we all need to look after number one above all else, so before you consider helping others with their mental health, it is important that you are well mentally. Helping others in a pickle when you are not well can cause harm to you and them. It can trigger a negative reaction from either party, which may well have knock-on effects on you and them.

If you cannot support someone, there are lots of organisations out there who will offer that person help. You can help by pointing them in the right direction (see the 'Helpful Resources' section towards the end of the book for some helpful examples).

How to help and what signs to look for

Although each person in need has different requirements, they fall into three broad categories in the early days, which are:

- People who want someone to listen to them and do not want answers or feedback, just reassurance that you are there for them.
- People who want someone to listen and respond with support and suggestions.
- People who want to talk but would prefer to talk about anything other than their scenario.

You are likely to find that conversations will often naturally lead to talking about what is troubling them, but you should not push them into sharing their issues. If it happens naturally, be careful to check regularly with the person, making sure they are happy to continue. Making them aware that you will talk about other things instead, if they prefer is very important.

For us to help someone who is struggling with their mental health, the first thing we need to do is to listen without judgement. Shame is a powerful driver for many people to be secretive and non-communicative about their feelings and the truth. They are highly likely to seem different to you. You should avoid telling them they have changed. They will know.

During the periods when I have needed support, there were few things I found harder to be reminded of than this.

Maybe they do not want to have changed. They may even have found that they are finally comfortable being who they truly want to be.

Our illnesses and our willingness to talk about them are only likely to be made worse by being reminded of how others think we should behave.

Accept and embrace the person in front of you, help them recover their way and at their pace.

Be aware of people's body language, observe their behaviour. Ask about their sleep patterns, observe how they are with you and other people. Is their body changing? Are their habits different from normal?

We humans have a built-in skill of observing others. Our instinct for these matters is normally pretty good, even when we are dealing with strangers. When people say that first impressions count, they really do.

Useful tips to keep in mind

Here are some useful tips that can help you support others when they are finding things hard:

1. Ask twice, are you OK? Are you sure?

2. If they are thinking of seeking medical help or going to a mental health group, or even taking up a new hobby, these things can be a lot easier with a comrade alongside. So maybe you could offer to go along with them?

3. Men often use insults towards one another disguised as humour to deflect emotional pain and shame. Pay close attention to language being used and what effect it may seem to have had. If you feel that someone may have been upset, you could check that they are OK.

4. Know where to seek help, offer numbers, helplines, chat support, etc. When someone is in a dark place, they may struggle to seek support. By leaving information or leaflets somewhere you know that they will find them, you may help them without them needing to know who left it. (see the 'Helpful Resources' section towards the end of the book for some helpful examples)

5. Self-care is vital, so be aware if people do not appear to be looking after themselves.

6. Suggest they establish routines. This was something that really helped me. Through my voluntary work, I have spoken to many people who feel they have given up; they don't get out of bed and they engage less and less in normal life. Making sure I ate breakfast, giving myself tasks to undertake and achieve, provided me with routine which became vital to my recovery.

7. Trust your instincts. This is something that can fail a person struggling with their mental health. They may need to 'borrow' yours.

8. Let them know they haven't failed, they are not at fault and that there is always a way forward.

9. Be willing to put up with some less than grateful behaviour. However, don't let it get out of hand; sometimes a reminder that they need to behave a certain way from someone they trust is what they need.

10. As a last resort, or when the time feels right, let them know that while you want to respect their confidence, if you're genuinely worried about their safety, you may need to involve the right people to ensure they get the support they need.

The Black Dog by Matthew Johnstone

The author and illustrator, Matthew Johnstone, has written several books and an animated cartoon which for me does a great job of demonstrating how it feels to become depressed and how a person can fall into depression without even being aware of it. It shows both someone who may suffer with depression and those around them, how it can affect a person.

It is a great honour when someone seeks you out to share their feelings with you. To keep their trust and continue to offer support, maintaining confidentiality is paramount. They have come to you because they believe in you and they trust you.

Chapter 24
News bulletins

NEWS bulletin #1 (January 2024)

Remember that I said I've never written a book before and that I have no idea how to go about it? Well, I'm basically letting it fall out onto the pages so that I can share my thoughts and experiences with you. Something else I thought I could do is share, at intervals throughout the book, the milestones connected to its development — and this is the first one.

It is January 2024 and I've just been speaking with a friend who has lost someone very dear to them — their brother, with whom they were extremely close. They said they felt terrible because they didn't believe they had the right to grieve as deeply as their brother's wife. That was not an angle I had ever considered before and I could see in this person (someone I've known for a long time and have great respect for) how much this was hurting them. And it was all because of love: for her brother and for his wife, who she also loved dearly.

My advice to my friend was that grief isn't a finite energy, there isn't a limited amount to go around. We all manage it differently and they were just as entitled to feel the pain and heartbreak of losing a loved one as anyone else. I also suggested that if their sister-in-law knew how much this was upsetting them, she would likely feel it was important that they grieve in whatever way they needed to. The shared knowledge of just how special the person had been to many people might even help them both. For me, this is such an important part of remembering: that someone's impact on the planet was powerful and positive.

Having only just written the 'Grief' section of this book, I shared my poem about my grandma with my friend. I thought it might be something they could consider doing themselves, or that it might inspire them to try something similar. It was the first piece I'd written for the book that I had shared with anybody. It felt scary, but it also felt lovely that it might help someone. I worried it might come across as a bit self-indulgent and not be useful to them, but they were very kind. They said it had helped, that they found it touching and that they could imagine us playing Monopoly in the sun together.

I was both excited and flattered to hear this feedback. It was the first little snapshot that showed me that I might be on to something, that writing this book might just help people, just as I'd hoped.

NEWS bulletin #2 (mid-March 2024)

Esther (my wife) has just read a really early draft, just short of ten thousand words and she thinks it's great. She said that she felt it was very readable and that she didn't want to put it down. If anyone was going to offer constructive criticism, it was Esther.

NEWS bulletin #3 (end of March 2024)

After hearing on the Chris Evans show that Penny Thresher, from the CarFest Buddies Facebook page, was a writing coach and editor, I sent her my book. She said I'm on the right track and much further ahead that most first-time writers she has come across. She knows the genre and the latest in that area and she doesn't think that there is another book out there like it and thinks it's a brilliant idea. I am very happy!

NEWS bulletin #4 (beginning of April 2024)

Penny says that she thinks the book is beautiful and it's seriously impressive stuff!! What a compliment. I'm buzzing with excitement.

NEWS bulletin #5 (mid-April 2024)

I'm six weeks into putting the book together and I have written just short of thirty-five thousand words. It is feeling like I have broken the back of writing this book and I can't quite believe how I have got here. I spent approximately eighteen months dreaming that I was going to write a book; I wrote a few hundred words in that time and then, boom, something clicked and here I am. Seriously putting what I have written into some kind of sensible order to be edited and published and hopefully so that I can have a copy in my hand for the August Bank Holiday 2024. The only problem is, I am feeling I may have another book in me!

NEWS bulletin #6 (early May 2024)

I'm having a wobble!!!!! I haven't done much with the book for just over a week as I have been away. I am conscious that I do not want to lose momentum. I don't know if it's my ADHD, but it is something to do with my make up that I have a habit of being obsessed with a thing (like the book) for around three to six months and once I have done it to death, I can drop it like a stone.

I have done this with diets, with exercise, hobbies, etc. But I have come so far now with the book that I can't afford to do it with this. I also think that the book is actually pretty good so far and may really benefit someone which is my ultimate goal. There are just so many twiddly bits that I am worried need attention, that it is overwhelming me a bit. I've put a message in to Penny, the editor, to say that I feel swamped and need her help to untangle myself a bit. It will be OK. I think……

NEWS bulletin #7 (mid-May 2024)

The message I sent to my editor:

"Hi Penny, I want to send you this before I hear from you about the transcript I sent you last week, so that you know that it's authentic. I am not chasing you, so please don't think that. When I sent you the book I was in a muddle. I felt so embroiled in it I was struggling to see the wood for the trees. Here's where it gets interesting. By passing it to you, knowing that it is in safe hands, it seemed to offer me the confidence and clarity to pick up and carry on. In the past week, I know that I have sorted lots of things out that have been bugging me. The book is tidier, easier to read and flows better. None of this means I have it sorted by any stretch of the imagination, but knowing that I had you on my side, working your informed magic, somehow gave me the confidence to do some of the heavy lifting which had weighed me down. So, I just wanted to thank you before you said how awful what I sent to you is."

NEWS bulletin #8 (late May 2024)

I've had a meeting with Penny, my editor. She has read the whole of the first draft, the first person to do this, not even I have done this in order. Penny says it's looking good and we can get started on the editing. She is keen to get the book out there, as she believes it is needed. How exciting is that!?!?!

NEWS bulletin #9 (early June 2024)

I read the section from **Chapter 2, 'Mental Health is for flaky people'** section to my friend 'Bob' and his daughter this weekend and he seemed pretty flattered. As a man who likes to talk, he had little to say, but he gave me a reassuring nod and he said that he approved of what I had written.

NEWS bulletin #10 (June 2024)

(as referred to in chapter 13)

I had a breakthrough this morning. As a child I would regularly get into trouble for doing something which I thought was helpful and I could not understand why. It could be really upsetting and frustrating, which added to the ADHD difficulties of managing my emotions.

The breakthrough I had was this: I was making some boiled eggs for breakfast (I'm trying to reduce my calorie intake). So I had three peeled boiled eggs sitting on a plate in the kitchen. I looked up and around the extractor fan near the ceiling, there were some dusty cobwebs, so I thought, "I know, I'll get the brush and get those now." I wandered off to get the brush and enroute realised that if I do that now I will cover my boiled eggs with dust and cobwebs.

It dawned on me at that point that, the times as a child when I had decided out of the blue to sweep something up outside but I left the back door open, so I filled the house with dust. Or a time when I thought that I would water the garden not realising that some plants didn't need a lot of water and killing them. My ADHD caused me to do things at a totally inappropriate time, or in a way that I have not appropriately thought out and to this day I have to manage this.

Despite this being and ADHD sufferer trying to do the right thing in the wrong way, I ask that we all try and keep this in mind when someone's intentions are good, but they do something which causes an issue.

NEWS bulletin #11 (mid July 2024)

Bad News! It doesn't look like I am going to make my August bank holiday target date for the promo print of the book. It was always a little ambitious, but I hoped I might just be able to do it. There is still a chance, but it is very low. I am now aiming for the print run to take place in Autumn, so fingers crossed for that, I suppose.

NEWS bulletin #12 (late July 2024)

I may have finally found a publishing company which suits my requirements. Publishing a book and arranging the links with the various sales outlets is like a dark art. It's such a minefield, so I'm pleased to have possibly found an organisation that will do the things I need them to.

NEWS bulletin #13 (early August 2024)

I've been looking into things to consider when marketing a book. One thing I have seen is do not waste money on business cards. Authors rarely hand them out and they don't really do much. I'm going to a festival at the end of August and as I won't have a copy of the book, I would like something to hand out, so I can discuss it with people and provide them with an easy way of registering their interest in a sneak peek at the book.

And then……. I had a brainwave…….. BOOKMARKS!!!

I have put together a bookmark with my details on and a QR code people can scan to register their interest!!! I know it might not sound like much, but I'm well excited. They've arrived and they are amazing!

NEWS bulletin #14 (August Bank Holiday 2024)

I have just arrived back after a six-and-a-half-hour drive from Laverstoke Park Farm, Near Overton in Hampshire (I had to stop for an hour long 'Nana nap' on my way home – I have never done this before – it was amazing!!). That is where CarFest is located. I have had a great weekend. The festival was great from a music and entertainment point of view and I could share the concept of this book with dozens of CarFesters, as well as several influential people in the field of health and wellbeing. The ideas behind my book were met with such positivity and I had lots of positive feedback. Not least for the title and the cover. That felt really nice. I also felt that some of those in the know could see that there was a need for the message I am trying to spread and that they were interested in seeing how it might go. Very exciting.

NEWS bulletin #15 (October 2024)

This week has been a real gut punch. I have always been dreading the publishing element of this process and despite making links in July with a publisher that seemed to suit me, I would be foolish if I did not look into other options too. This week I got a quote back from a publisher and it was as follows:

£2600 for setup costs (this is me doing things on a budget I could have easily spent a lot more, particularly if I was not able to provide the images etc. that I have as part of my book.)

Ordering one thousand books at a total cost of £3058.00 (making each book £3.058)

The publisher recommended a price range of up to £13.99. I decided upon £12.95, to try and keep it affordable for people.

If sold on Amazon, they charge 60% of the total price of the book, which works out at £7.77 per book.

The publisher in question then take a further fee of 15% of the total price of the book which works out at £1.94425 per book.

If you have been following closely, you will see that this leaves £0.18 for me to share with the charities, the tax man and me to try and cover the costs already charged by the publisher. Just to put that in context I would need to sell over 40,000 books in order to be able to cover all of the publishing costs.

In this country there are around 3,000 new books published each week. Not many of those books sell many copies and the response from the publisher to my concerns over the above figures was that I should encourage people not to buy through Amazon as this is the worst case. Whether you like it or not most books are purchased through Amazon. What this does teach us though, is when you are considering buying a book, if you truly want to support the author, it would be kind of you to seek out their website or the website of their publisher and buy it from them, as this will see that the majority of the profits reach the right people.

Because of all of this it has been back to the drawing board, so that I can publish this book for people and maximise the value of it for the charities and to try and cover my costs, so that I can consider writing the other books I have in mind.

Hopefully the fact that you are reading this means that I managed it.

NEWS bulletin #16 (November 2024)

Ok, I've had my tantrum and the proverbial slap across the face I needed from my wife and friends basically telling me to pull myself together and get on with it. I've come too far to let this hiccup stop me. So, on advice from experts, I have spent the last couple of weeks putting together a synopsis to submit to a literary agent, for their feedback and the possibility that they might just accept my work and run with it.

What I can tell you is that to those of you who think writing a book is hard, it is NOTHING compared to writing a synopsis of a book. It's a truly awful thing to have to do, totally outside of my comfort zone. But it's finally done and submitted, so fingers crossed we can beat the 18p scenario from the last Newsflash.

NEWS bulletin #17 (January 2025)

I have now submitted applications to 26 different literary agents/agencies I am really excited and hopeful that one or even better, some of them will see the benefits that this book has to offer. It really is quite a painful process to submit the information to the various agencies, each one has slightly different requirements, some want a chapter of your choice, some want the first two. Some want a description of the book, information about me, some want to know what competition exists out there and ask how this book measures up against it.

I have everything crossed, but I am going to need some staying power as most say that they may take eight to twelve weeks before the come back to people and worse than that many say that they may not come back to me at all!!!

NEWS bulletin #18 (April 2025)

Well, nobody can say that it isn't through a lack of trying. I have now heard back from six of the twenty six literary agencies I approached and I think it is unlikely that I am going to hear back from any more. I have some loose ends that I would like to tidy up with this book, things I had left in such a way that if an agent wanted to change them we could with relative ease and things like these final Bulletin updates on the process of writing the book.

I feel now that I have exhausted the opportunities available to me that would provide professional help to produce this book within my budget. My book which has been all but finished for nine months now, is eagerly awaited by many and I do not want to keep it back for any longer. Although I have never wanted to, it would seem that the only way I have left available to me which will see this book published soon and within my budget, is if I go ahead and do it online.

I have also had my first proper review of the book, by a lovely Canadian lady whose identity I will keep anonymous. But here it is:

"Reading your book made me feel seen, supported and less alone. Mental health has always felt like such a taboo topic, so it's refreshing to hear honest stories through your podcast and book. I'm really grateful for that."

- Anonymous Early Reader

Given that my book is written by me, a British Northern Orangutan and I can only share the benefit of my own experience as a working class bloke. I'm pretty chuffed with that. So much so, that you may have noticed it's now on the cover too!

NEWS bulletin #19 (June 2025)

I have actually ordered the proof copies, and they arrived yesterday. It makes things so real. However it has also highlighted gazillions of errors and changes that need to be made. So it's nose to the grindstone for Esther and me. Esther is going through each page with a pencil and marking the things that need attending to. Then I frantically go through what she's done and make changes to the electronic copy.

It's mainly little things, but there are lots of them. I want this book to be as good as it possibly can be by the time it goes to print. I want to show people that this daft northern lad with ADHD, a full time job and too many hobbies can write a book of some worth. If that means doing it alone (with my wife's help) then so be it. After we have tidied it up, it will be getting submitted. I'd like to have it ready before the end of the month as it's men's mental health awareness month which seems quite fitting. So, I'll see you on the other side. Thanks for getting this far, and if you started at the back then you're a bloody cheat, but I'm still grateful.

Chapter 25

Your worksheets

In this chapter you will find blank copies of the worksheets I have given examples of throughout the book. These are for your use, you can write directly on them and keep them to help you to recognise and maintain matters that we have discussed in this book. You can also visit **www.pieeatingman.co.uk** where you can order additional electronic and hard copy workbooks for your use moving forward.

Remember these are yours, you can write whatever you feel to be appropriate on them, you do not have to share them with other people, but perhaps, when you feel comfortable enough you will have a record of your feelings and thoughts that you can share if you wish.

My Life Pivots

Description of life pivot	When it happened?	How things changed

Use this worksheet to reflect on your current mental health state. As mentioned in **Chapter 5 – My mental health.**

Depression Diary		
Symptom	Date	Length of time

A simple tool to track moods, habits and thoughts related to depression as mentioned in **Chapter 8 – Depression**.

Date	Time	Place	Who where you with?	The cause of stress & how it made you feel	Stress rating score (Low 1 - 10 High)			Stress Period (Hrs/mins)
					Before	During	After	

Capture stressful events and identify common triggers. As mentioned in **Chapter 9 – Stress** and **Chapter 12 – Trauma and triggers**.

	List of Change Indicators	
		Y/N
		Y/N
		Y/N
		Y/N
		Y/N
		Y/N
		Y/N
		Y/N
		Y/N
		Y/N
		Y/N

Record moments of anxiety, possible causes and strategies for relief. As mentioned in **Chapter 10 – Anxiety**.

List of Change Indicators

Have I had too much sleep?	Y/N
Have I had enough sleep?	Y/N
Have I eaten enough healthy food?	Y/N
Has my diet changed? How?	Y/N
Am I hungry?	Y/N
Am I thirsty?	Y/N
Am I unwell?	Y/N
Has the weather changed? (hot/cold?)	Y/N
Have I taken medication?	Y/N
Have I had alcohol?	Y/N
Have I used recreational drugs?	Y/N

Helps build consistency and structure for recovery. As mentioned in **Chapter 16 – Maintaining good mental health** and **Chapter 17 – Healthy routines**.

Date	Three things I'm grateful for today
	1.
	2.
	3.
	1.
	2.
	3.
	1.
	2.
	3.
	1.
	2.
	3.
	1.
	2.
	3.

Log daily gratitude, acts of kindness or forgiveness. As mentioned in **Chapter 18 – Kindness, gratitude & forgiveness**.

Life time Bucket List

A personal template for setting long term goals and dreams. As mentioned in **Chapter 20 – Goals, bucket lists & plans**.

Bucket List Items achieved

A personal template for recalling goals and dreams achieved. As mentioned in **Chapter 20 – Goals, bucket lists & plans**.

Bucket List item	Revisit and why

A personal template for recalling goals and dreams achieved. As mentioned in **Chapter 20 – Goals, bucket lists & plans**

My Pros & Cons

Pro's	Con's

Use this worksheet to explore your personal strengths and weaknesses. As mentioned in **Chapter 21 – Toolkit for a healthy mind**.

My Joy & Worry Lists	
What brings me joy & Relaxation?	What brings me anxiety Worry & Distress?

Reflective prompts to increase self-awareness. As mentioned in **Chapter 22 – Getting to know you and helping yourself**.

Chapter 26
I did a thing!!!
(with a little help from my friends)

Well, I could be wrong but seems that I have actually done it. I have written a book! As of this moment, I have no idea how good it is. I have only shown it to a handful of people, but they speak highly of it and I admit, that feels nice. No matter what the popularity or outcome of this book, my main driver remains the same. If the information I have shared helps one person, my job has been successful.

Writing the book has also been extremely good for my soul. It has helped me to exorcise matters from my past and to exercise mindfulness muscles in ways that have been extremely helpful and supportive to my development on this journey.

I must thank some people who have helped me along the way in formulating and writing this book.

The first person I need to thank is you, the reader. Thank you for trusting me enough for you to buy, borrow, or find this book and read it to this point.

The next person I must thank is my wife Esther, for so many reasons! I would need to write another book in order to capture them all. She helped me on my mental health journey and she has been unendingly supportive throughout all my hare-brained schemes over the years, not least this one. Esther is my best the extra pair of hands and eyes could not have done without when producing the book.

I need to thank my mum for doing such a sterling job of raising me; I am not perfect, but that's not her fault.

I must thank my editor Penny Thresher for her support both personally and professionally, it's one thing to type a book out on a laptop using Microsoft Word, it is another thing entirely for that to be made readable by the average man on the Clapham omnibus and then to be wrestled into a form which is pleasing to the reader's eye and then published. I would still be very much lost in this labyrinth without Penny's kindness and breadth of knowledge.

I need to thank my friend Mark Wogan, who, knowingly or unknowingly, has been inspiring and supportive during the writing of this book, offering his Home Slice Pizza and advice as an experienced coach; along with his razor-sharp wit when it was required, but not always anticipated.

I need to thank Chris Evans and the Virgin Breakfast Show team at Virgin Radio as well as Ryan Tubridy and Eddie Temple Morris and the CarFest team; they have been a wellness support and inspiration every day. Without Chris and CarFest I probably would not have taken this any further than a pipe dream.

Suzy Izzard must also get a mention, for the time she offered me, the advice she gave me and the kick up the arse she provided when it was most needed.

Dr Rangan Chatterjee for his words of encouragement and Bryony Gordon for twisting my arm and giving me the courage to keep the menopause chapter included in the book.

Our lovely friends Tony and Sue Lovejoy, for agreeing to review and be honest about potentially contentious content in the book. Your advice has been critical.

Finally, everyone who has kindly supported me along this journey, friends, family, colleagues (many of whom are friends too), the **www.myblackdog.co** pack, who have not only given me support, but the charity also helped me to see the need for this book.

The book I originally set out to write is not the book I have ultimately ended up writing. There are elements in there, but the writing process was such that the content just "fell out of my head" onto the page. It was the right time for me to write this book and it shaped itself. As a result, there's a chance that the original idea for the book is still in this walnut rattling around inside my noggin. We will have to see.

The End, at least for now.

Chapter 27
The photos

Let's be honest you looked at them before you got to the part of the book they refer to. Don't worry I would have done exactly the same thing.

Photo 1 - Me with Chris Evans asking Suzy Izzard "How do you write a book?" CarFest 2022, in front of the 15-20,000 strong crowd

(photograph courtesy of Duncan Cowley, who by pure chance took a picture of the situation and shared it online – not my best side Duncan).

Photo 2 - Me at the very wet CarFest (North) 2022

Photo 3 -Meeting Suzy Izzard at the My Black Dog stand at CarFest 2023, shortly before I was given my reality check.

Photo 4 - Chris Evans & me at CarFest North, July 2022, this is exactly when the idea for this book was spawned.

Photo 5 - Me climbing my first palm tree at 7 years old, July 1987.

Photo 6 - The breathtaking marine life, living around a coral pinnacle, Shark/Yolanda Reef, Ras Mohamed National Park, Egypt June 2023 (I'm afraid you'll have to imagine the colours).

Photo 7 – Day one of my current job, Oct 2004. This guy is still unwell, look at those dark eyes!

Photo 8 - My self-portrait at age 26. Unconsciously I knew how unwell I still was.

Photo 9 - Kevin and me in the Car Park before setting off to Mosedale Bothy, June 2013

Photo 10 – After seeing my first shark in the Red Sea June 2023 (this is the underwater signal for shark)

Photo 11 - Chris Evans surprised me when he pulled me out of the crowd to talk about my beard shave, in front of thousands of people. CarFest 2023.

Photo 12 - Chris Evans and me in the Virgin Radio Studio immediately after my beard shave, Dec 2023 – I look like a Mole Rat crossed with a potato on this pic.

Photo13 - My Awesome Family

Chapter 28
Helpful resources

Below is a list of charities and organisations which may be able to offer support to people for some of the issues discussed in this book.

Advisory, Conciliation and Arbitration Service (ACAS)

ACAS helps anyone who needs employment law or workplace advice, including employers, employees and workers.

They provide confidential, free advice on:
- any work-related problem or question you have
- what the law says and how it relates to you
- good practice at work

- your options, including any risks and benefits

You do not have to give any personal details.

Helpline 0300 123 1100

Alcoholics Anonymous (AA)

Alcoholics Anonymous help each other and support people. They make sure that you are not alone. Together, they help to find strength and hope.

Free phone: 0800 9177650

Email: help@aamail.org

Chatbox: www.alcoholics-anonymous.org.uk

Andy's man club

Andy's man club is a mental health support charity supporting men who are struggling with their mental health.

Andrew (Andy) Roberts, a twenty-three-year-old man, tragically took his own life. None of his family or friends had any idea that he was struggling with his mental health.

Andy's mother and his brother-in-law setup Andy's Man club to bring together men who may not otherwise be comfortable discussing their feelings. They now have over one hundred groups across the UK who meet every Monday evening and create a judgment-free, confidential space where men over the age of eighteen can speak with their peers about any difficulties they may be experiencing.

Their motto is that at no time do they want to leave

#thatoneman to suffer; and #ItsOKtoTalk; helping men see that the next day has the possibility of being better than this one.

Info@andysmanclub.co.uk

www.andysmanclub.co.uk

Visit and find your local group

Cruse bereavement support

Offer support through their website, national helpline, group, zoom, telephone or one-to-one in person support. They aim to make sure everyone grieving gets the help they need in a way that works for them. They have a specially trained dedicated team of 4,000 bereavement volunteers.

Helpline: 08088081677

Campaign Against Living Miserably (CALM)

CALM is a suicide prevention charity fighting to reduce the devastating impact of suicide in the UK. They run a life-saving helpline for anyone affected by suicide or suicidal thoughts. It's free, anonymous and open from 5pm to midnight.

Men's sheds

Connection, conversation and creation – that's what

joining a Men's Shed is all about.

Men's Sheds encourage people to come together to make, repair and repurpose, supporting projects in their local communities. Improving wellbeing, reducing loneliness and combatting social isolation.

Search for a local Shed to join below:

www.menssheds.org.uk

info@menssheds.org.uk

Local authority health and wellbeing services

Social Prescribing is a service which is usually made available through Local Authorities and medical services. They offer an extensive list of self-help solutions and service referrals designed to help people find their own path to living a happy and well life. Signposting to local healthy body and mind resources is typically available online. You may also find that there are links to relevant local charities, clubs and support networks which suit you. For more information you can search the internet for Social Prescribing services local to your area.

Mental Health Mates (MHM)

Mental Health Mates is a nationwide network of volunteer-led, peer support groups that encourage people to get moving and talking for their mental health. Groups across the UK regularly meet to walk, connect and share without fear or judgement. With over one hundred Walks across the UK and more being added every day, there are plenty of wonderful Walks to join! Search for a walk near you using the information below:

www.mentalhealthmates.co.uk

hello@mentalhealthmates.co.uk

Mind

An organisation which offers support to people struggling with their mental health in a number of different ways. They empower people to understand their mental health and the choices available to them. They do this through a number of supportive ways.

Contact number 111 option 2 for not emergency support. This service can be busy

Support line 0300 102 1234

Info line 0300 123 3393

Welfare benefits Line 0300 222 5782

Legal Line 0300 466 6463

www.mind.org.uk

My Black Dog (MBD)

A peer-to-peer chat-based system for people who were struggling with their mental health. All of their volunteers had a history of their own mental health problems and they offer advice and a friendly ear to anyone who wants to come onto their online chat system.

Visit: www.myblackdog.co and start a chat

Narcotics Anonymous (NA)

If you have a problem with drugs, NA are recovering drug addicts who can help you get and stay clean. They hold over 1000 meetings a week in the UK. representing a lot of addicts, helping them to stay clean. They have vast resources of experience to draw upon.

Free phone: 0300 9991212 (10am – 00:00am)

Suicide prevention UK

Suicide Prevention UK is an award-winning Suicide Prevention charity.

They help anyone who may be struggling with their mental health and/or thoughts of suicide. Their volunteers use their skills, training and empathetic approach to offer a non-judgemental listening ear to help people. Their volunteers aim to signpost individuals to the most relevant support available to them to get them the help they deserve.

Free phone: 0800 6895652 (24hr)

Samaritans

If you urgently need support, please contact the emergency services. If you need someone to speak with, please call Samaritans – 116123 or text SHOUT to 85258 for dedicated text support.

THERE ARE MANY MORE CHARITIES AND SUPPORT NETWORKS AVAILABLE, SOME LOCAL, SOME REGIONAL AND SOME NATIONAL. JUST SEARCH THE INTERNET FOR YOUR SPECIFIC QUERY AND HELP SHOOULD BE AVAILABLE.

Glossary of 'Woo Woo' words and terms used in this book

The language of mental health can be confusing and off-putting, with lots of terminology which some might not be familiar with. We've put together this glossary to help you understand things a little better.

A

Attention Deficit Disorder (ADHD)
A mental health condition which can cause people to be restless and impatient. People with ADHD can struggle to concentrate and often act impulsively.

Agoraphobia
A fear of being in a place or situation where you feel you can't escape or where help might not be available if you become anxious.

Antidepressants

A type of medicine used to treat depression. They're sometimes prescribed for other health problems such as chronic pain and for other mental health conditions such as anxiety or obsessive-compulsive disorder.

Anxiety

A range of mental and physical states, mainly arising from being consciously worried about the future, or afraid of an actual situation. It's a normal human response to lots of situations, but if it's persistent or out of proportion to the situation, it can be a symptom of poor mental health.

B

Bipolar disorder

A mental health condition that causes repeated, severe mood swings. At different times, mood can vary from excitement and elation (called mania) to depression and despair.

C

Centring (ourselves)

Is the act of bringing our emotions and feelings back to where they should be and where we feel most comfortable. If we are not centred, we may have become out of touch with how we operate when calm and comfortable.

Clasper

The male reproductive organs of sharks and other fish.

Cognitive Behavioural Therapy (CBT)

A type of talking therapy that can help to change negative patterns in how you think, feel and behave. It's an effective therapy for many types of mental health problems, including depression and anxiety.

Come Down

The unpleasant symptoms associated with the period after a person has used drugs, alcohol, etc. to achieve an artificial high. The symptoms can affect mood, motivation, energy levels and even diet.

Complementary therapies

Methods which try to treat illnesses and fall outside of conventional medicine. Some therapies claim to treat mental health conditions. These include mediation, reflexology, acupuncture, aromatherapy and Yoga, to name but a few.

Counselling

A type of talking therapy where a trained therapist listens to what you have to say and then helps you to deal with your emotional issues.

Cyberbullying

Bullying via mobile phone or online (for example email, social networks and instant messenger), unlike traditional bullying, cyberbullying can mean that people experience bullying in places where they should otherwise be safe. Cyberbullying and traditional bullying can take place at the same time.

D

Depression

A condition where you have a continuous low mood and/or a loss of interest and enjoyment in your life.

Diagnosis

When a doctor identifies a condition based on signs, symptoms and test results.

E

Emotional Intelligence (EQ)

I the act of being self-aware, of one's own emotions, other people's emotions and having the ability to alter yours to respond appropriately and positively to theirs. It requires the ability to empathise and be socially aware. It requires the ability to regulate your own emotions and adapt them to the circumstances as required.

G

Gas lighting

Gas lighting is a form of psychological abuse which can cause a person to question a version of events, their memories, their sanity and their perception of reality. Carried out by a person manipulating the truth or belittling the opinions and thoughts of a person to be trivial or petty when they are not. Gas lighting is a common form of domestic abuse.

Gender Bias

This is simply the giving of preference to one gender over another. Gender Bias can be conscious and unconscious. Unconscious gender bias can be a serious stumbling block towards gender equality. Many societies include a gender bias and more often than not it shows preference towards men.

GP (General Practitioner)

A local doctor who can treat all common medical conditions and refer patients to hospitals and other medical services for urgent and specialist treatment.

H

Honey badger

Honey Badgers are found in Africa. They look like badgers and are a member of the weasel family. They are renowned for their willingness to be aggressive and fearless when defending themselves, even against animals much larger than themselves. They have a reputation which precedes them, and it is that they are alleged to target the testicles when they attack, although this is an urban legend. Having said that, I will not be testing the theory.

I

Insomnia

A condition where you find it difficult getting to sleep or staying asleep for long enough to feel refreshed the next morning.

Isolation

Isolation, or social isolation, means having a low level of social contact in your daily life. It can increase your risk of poor mental health.

M

Mania

An energetic mood of excitement and elation. It is a symptom of bipolar disorder.

Manifestation

The process of focussing thoughts and intentions on a specific goal or outcome, in order for them to become reality.

Meditation

An ancient 'mind-body' practice used to increase calmness and enhance overall wellbeing. Has some similarities with mindfulness.

Micromanagement

Is a management style where a supervisor or manager over scrutinises processes and decisions being made by staff.

Mindfulness

A practice that helps people tame their thoughts and feelings. It combines the awareness of ourselves and the environment around us and our need to pay attention to the present moment without judgement. Many mental health practices encourage the use of mindfulness techniques alongside their specific purpose.

O

Obsessive-Compulsive Disorder (OCD)
A condition where you have obsessive thoughts or compulsive behaviours (things you feel you must do) or both.

P

Panic attack
A period of severe fear and overwhelming physical feelings.

Phobia
An extreme form of anxiety or fear of a specific object or situation, which is out of proportion to the actual threat or danger the situation poses.

Post-Traumatic Stress Disorder (PTSD)
A condition that affects people who have experienced or witnessed a highly traumatic or catastrophic event.

Being present
To be present is to understand where you are both physically, mentally and even spiritually, how you feel, how the world around you feels at that moment. It normally infers that you are comfortable and content with the scenario you are in.

Psychiatrist
A medical doctor who specialises in the diagnosis, treatment and prevention of mental health conditions.

R

Relapse

When a condition that appeared to have improved or gone away comes back.

Relaxation techniques

Things you can do yourself to try to relax and manage stressful situations.

S

Self-help

This can be a 'light-touch' self-guided treatment prescribed by your doctor. Or it can refer to a more general self-guided approach to looking after your mental wellbeing day-to-day.

Stress

How you feel and respond when life puts you under a lot of pressure. It's not a mental health condition itself, but stress can increase your risk of poor mental health.

Symptoms

Evidence or a sign of a health condition that the person with the condition notices themselves. An example for mental health might be low mood.

T

Talking therapies

A type of treatment that involves talking to a trained professional about your feelings. This may help you feel better if you're going through a difficult time.

Tasmanian Devil

The Tasmanian Devil is a stocky, carnivorous marsupial. They reach around 12Kgs in size and have powerful jaws and much greater levels of aggression than their size might suggest.

Toxic masculinity

A phrase used to describe the negative impact of the preference and bias offered to men and masculinity within cultures. It is a phrase used to refer to the oppression of women, although its impact affects the whole of society.

Trauma

An extremely upsetting, stressful, or threatening situation.

Treatment

Something that aims to reduce or remove the symptoms of a mental health condition.

Triggers

Events that influence someone to react in a certain way. Knowing your triggers can assist you in working towards managing them and how you react to them. The understanding and management of triggers is a useful tool in personal mental health management.

W

Woo-woo

Based on beliefs or ethereal influences, as opposed to scientific discovery or knowledge, these may include complimentary therapies and therapies which originate from astrological beliefs, for example.

The encore

As I have already mentioned, the earliest foundations of this book were laid at CarFest in 2022. Since that time Chris Evans and the Breakfast Show team have supported my charity efforts and they have been supportive of the writing of this book.

Because of this, it is very important to me that a percentage of the profits generated from the sale of this book are donated to the CarFest Charities. Without CarFest, Chris Evans and other contacts I have made through CarFest like my festi besties Jo and Alice, Penny from Cornerhouse words and the sage that is Mark Wogan the book would not exist to help you.

Since its inception, CarFest has raised over £25 million in donations to children's charities and My Black Dog. The team behind CarFest work tirelessly to create what I believe is the best family festival in the country. I have seen firsthand the difference this event makes to people's lives and the year-round work that the staff and volunteers do, does not go unnoticed.

Thank you for taking the time to read my book. I hope it has helped you or someone you love. If you think it has, I would dearly love to hear from you.

You can contact me by emailing me at pieeatingman@outlook.com. It would be lovely to receive your feedback.

You never know, it might just be enough to spur me on to writing another book in the future…MIGHT.

If you have enjoyed this book, why not have a listen to my Podcast 'Chewing the Crust with The Pie Eating Man'. Every two weeks I speak to amazing people with amazing stories in which they have overcome obstacles and difficulties and gone on to live life to the fullest, showing us all that life is well worth working at and living to the max and even so we have something of a responsibility to.

Chewing the Crust is available on YouTube, Spotify, iTunes and Amazon or wherever you get your podcasts and it's well worth a listen to the tales of these remarkable people - You will see that Superheroes truly do walk among us!

About the author

The Pie Eating Man is an everyday individual who has spent the last twenty-five years navigating and managing his mental health challenges. Diagnosed with ADHD as an adult, he also deals with depression on a daily basis.

Throughout his journey, he has observed a significant gap in the understanding, appreciation and accessibility of wellness and mental health support for the average person. This is something he is passionate about changing, using a blend of humour and honesty to make these topics more approachable.

As a strong advocate for normalising mental health issues within society, he is dedicated to advancing the conversation around wellness. His goal is to explore and promote mental well-being for everyone, everywhere, in a way that resonates with their unique needs.

Printed in Dunstable, United Kingdom